Contents

POWERFUL LIFE SKILLS

FOR TEENS & YOUNG ADULTS

AN ESSENTIAL GUIDE

**How To Build True Confidence,
Achieve Healthy Habits, Manage Money Like a Pro
& Successfully Create Your Dream Life**

Lindsey Goodwin

POWERFUL LIFE SKILLS Worksheets

Scan the QR Code / Visit the Link
For Your Free Worksheets!

infinitelearning.ck.page/powerfullifeskills

Print them out and use them as a bookmark
so they're handy for Chapters 3, 4, 5, 12, 13 and 14.

This book is dedicated to all of you out there with a desperate desire to have the power to enjoy your life. I'm one of you. Let's do just that.

Introduction

Your Powerful Future Starts Here

"Life is either a daring adventure or nothing at all..."
                                        -Helen Keller

In this world of infinite possibilities, the transition to adulthood is both a challenging and exciting journey to experience. Venturing into the realm of adult choices can feel like a wild, mysterious dream that's difficult to make sense of. You may feel a mix of emotions - eagerness to claim your independence, anticipation for fun new experiences, some concern about money, coursework, bosses, or making new friends. You're not alone in these feelings, and don't have to prepare for these new experiences solo!

In this book you'll find guidance on boosting self-esteem, fostering relationships, managing your hard-earned cash, choosing your goals, and more. It has the answers to those questions keeping you up at night! It's going to spark your inspiration and fuel your ideas - your dreams for the future!

"But why *this* book? and "Who are *you* to be my guide?" you wonder. I'm so glad you asked.

This book, because with it you're getting both a companion and a map, ready to guide you through the maze of adulting with success. It's not just any book - you have the accumulated knowledge of a fellow traveler and coach in your grasp. Not only do I offer seemingly endless tools and advice, but support built on experience, empathy and understanding.

I can be your guide because I love coaching, I'm living my powerful dream life, and my entire goal for this book is to help you truly understand why *you* are powerful, and how to create *your* dream life too. You might wonder what exactly I mean, and how exactly you'll achieve this.

I mean that I have developed enough healthy self-confidence to *truly know* that I am powerful. And because I *know* that I am powerful, with choices I make I consider the questions: "Does this align with my hopes and intentions? Will this choice empower my dream life's continued creation and enjoyment?" Because I know that the answers matter, that I have the power to choose, and that my choices will either decrease my power, or increase it.

The power to live this way has resulted in an immense amount of personal wealth and helped me achieve many dreams for my life. I rock a multitude of healthy habits and use tools to avoid unhealthy behaviors, like negative self-talk and spiraling into anxiety. I understand how to take care of myself and live with gratitude. Helping others to master these skills is my joy and life's purpose. In this book I'll elaborate on the powerful skills you can master to create a powerful dream life of your own.

Now you might wonder, "What life skills are so powerful they can help me create my dream life? It's too good to be true!"

Please read on, my friend.

My growth in personal power has been made possible because I've constantly sought to learn new things that will interest or benefit me. I've been able to continuously learn new things because, at various points early on in my life, I came to understand the three most powerful life skills: *courage, curiosity, and creativity*.

Courage involves your emotions- your willingness to force yourself to face frightening or mysterious new ideas, experiences, or outcomes despite the protest of your mind or body. *Curiosity* involves your thoughts- your desire for and openness to new ideas, experiences, and outcomes. *Creativity* involves the two- your emotions and thoughts blended together leads to new ideas, experiences, and outcomes.

Some people believe, "These aren't skills, they're traits!"

Nonsense. Skills can be learned. Can you learn to have more courage, to be more curious, or more creative? You absolutely can. If anyone tells you otherwise, please do yourself and all of us a favor and just throw that belief in the garbage.

Now I'm not saying these three are the only essential skills in life. There's a kajillion fantastic life skills to make use of. Resourcefulness, patience, accounting know-how, responding versus reacting, thinking with clarity, speaking with intention, writing with creativity, just to name a few. All skills! But all of these truly involve at least one of the powerful three I mentioned before. Try naming a powerful life skill that doesn't require a bit of mastery of at least one of those three. You'll be hard-pressed to find one. That's why I call them "the powerful three".

By experiencing the magic and outcomes these three skills helped me achieve, I practiced them relentlessly, and built a solid foundation within myself that I could launch new dreams from again and again. I've been able to explore countless callings, travel around the world, and form precious relationships. I know the ups and downs of being a child caregiver, an animal educator, an aquarium hobbyist, a PADI student, a licensed hair styling professional, a wilderness trekker, a waitress, a tutor, a working student, a lab manager, an event and community coordinator, a financial assistant, an HR assistant, an author, and a life coach. In this last one, I've found my dream job.

Understanding the real value of courage, curiosity, creativity, and cementing my habit of using them daily, also allowed me to understand the importance of two other skills: critical thinking and research. These skills also fuel my motivation, determination, and accomplishment of dreams.

I'll be expanding on all of this in Chapter 1, and I think you'll enjoy it. Until then, let's hold that thought and shift gears back to the concept of creating your dream life!

What does your dream life look like? The ability to envision one varies greatly from person to person. For some, it includes a stable, predictable job; for others, it's freedom of movement or even opportunities to travel the world. For still others, it's meaningful friendships, freedom of thought and self-expression, or more time for passion projects. The common denominator in these desires is doing things we enjoy because they make us feel happy, fulfilled, and at peace. I'm sure you've heard the age-old wisdom that time is the most precious resource. Why? We want more *time* spent feeling happy, fulfilled, and at peace!

So what's a winning strategy for creating your dream life? Yep, spending more time doing what you enjoy! Bonus points if you guessed this part: If you do more of what you enjoy in your paid employment, much more of your life is spent living your dream. When you routinely execute healthy habits that allow you to feel happier and fulfilled, you'll be living your dream. When you master respect for yourself and others enough to consistently seek rewarding actions and interactions, you'll be living your dream. When you explore, choose and get to use knowledge gained from an educational program that brings you satisfaction and happiness, you'll be living your dream.

Some will protest. "But life isn't a walk in the park." "Life can be hellacious!" "My dreams must be too numerous or impossible to achieve from where I started, with the bummer hand I was dealt."

Here is the thing. Yes, we have incredible, powerful imaginations. Insatiable desires. Brilliant creativity. Infinite experiences we'd like to make real, lived memories. That is part of the nature of being human. Do we all have more dreams to bring to life? Of course we do. But the harder truth we need to come to terms with is that without learning to value our time as our most precious resource and without mastering powerful skills, we will most definitely not create our dream lives. To create our dream lives, we must embrace time as our most precious resource and master powerful skills.

So many people have told me they would have loved a person, or a book, to have given them more real-life advice for the range of situations they could expect journeying into adulthood. They would have loved to receive more guidance and tools on how to deal with life's challenges. Examples of ways to approach, understand, and resolve different problems. Like them, I wish I had found a collection of wisdom at my fingertips in the form of a compact, factual, and digestible book.

So, I realized that this book was something I wanted to create as a part of my own professional journey.

You'll notice along the way that I'll often interchange terms like school, educational program, training course, trade school, college, and work, to illustrate points about these options and experiences. Please know this is intentional. This book contains valuable information on college options and decisions and college life. Still, these are just a smaller part of a greater whole. The wealth of knowledge in this book comes from the fact that its insights and advice apply to a range of educational and life experiences. I myself have attended a trade school, training programs, colleges, and taken CLEP exams. This is why I'm able and eager to share with you on all of these topics, and provide the most relevant information.

Another disclaimer: This book does not include deep details of my personal life. It could not possibly, and does not contain, descriptions of all of the ups and downs I experienced through my teen and young adult years: the excitement, joy, struggles, love, anger, frustration, despair, determination, confusion, self-doubt, fear, break-throughs, and priceless moments. This book isn't about all that. Perhaps another day.

This book provides advice on the most essential, ever-important topics: Healthy habits! Education and learning! Creativity! Positive mindset, financial savvy, social skills, gaining life experience, working for a living, and more. It is that book I wish I had as a teen. It's the voice I wish I'd heard. A voice of wisdom, encouragement, knowledge, and unconditional love. A supportive companion to navigate future adventures.

So, if you find yourself feeling the thrill of the unknown or the dread of the uncertain, remember this: In this life-altering book, you have a map for navigating the realm of adulting and a mentor who understands the challenges and triumphs of the journey.

Included with this book are worksheets with enriching activities. These worksheets are opportunities for intentional self-discovery and growth. They will empower you to navigate your life purposefully, making choices that reflect who you are and who you want to become. Feel free to print, complete, save, and return to these as you embark on your adventures, using them to lead you toward success, fulfillment, and the realization of your aspirations.

Remember that every page turned is a step closer to unlocking the secrets of adulthood. You're gaining insights into some of life's complexities and nuances to enhance your life journey. But don't just take my word for it. Immerse yourself in these pages, and see what you learn. So let's plunge into the exciting pool of adulting, and learn about powerful life skills!

Go on, say it with me: "I am powerful! I am creating my dream life."

PART I

Taking Seriously Powerful
Care of Yourself

Chapter 1
The Power Of Critical Thinking and Research

> *"A great many people think they are thinking*
> *when they are merely rearranging their prejudices."*
>
> *-William James*

Before each of the new educational experiences and new jobs I've taken on, I've felt nervous, excited, and anxious about whether my abilities would be "up to snuff". But I've also embraced that they were fresh new chances to explore new interests and skills, gain confidence, and learn how to plan, write and think more efficiently.

Remember when I mentioned critical thinking and research, and said I would talk more about it in this chapter? Happy to have you here for it, my brilliant friend! I shared that courage, curiosity, and creativity helped me by their own merits, but they also brought me to a place of awe and understanding about critical thinking and research skills. I shared that like "the powerful three", critical thinking and research skills are also powerful tools for motivation, determination, and achieving dreams.

So here we are. This is the chapter where you'll take the deepest dive into parts of my personal journey of adulting. Because another part of building your dream life is having help, I need to share with you key moments I received help of my own. Because of that help, I was able to make seriously savvy financial, educational, and experiential decisions. So I can't emphasize the importance of powerful life skills without putting them in the context of my personal story. It would feel uh, rude!

You will have help too. Whether it's help you can see now, or help you haven't bumped into yet, put yourself out there with courage, curiosity and creativity, and I promise you, you will get it!

Shall we? The most pivotal moments in my early educational journey went something like this:

After high school, I enrolled in a 10-month trade school for cosmetology and earned my license. I worked as a hairstylist for 7 years - what a ride! It is a highly social and creative profession that I enjoyed and learned tons from. During the first two years I made money, experienced more of life, met interesting people from different backgrounds, "played therapist", expressed my creativity, and made people feel good. I also grew stronger in my independence. After those two years, I became more curious about other skillsets, knowledge, and college programs. There came a time when I felt in my gut and heart that I wanted to at least try my hand at college, to see if it was for me.

I ultimately decided to reduce my work as a hairstylist to part-time and enroll at a community college full-time. I wanted to see what a full course load felt like and how much I could handle, while also working a paid job. One of my clients recommended I start out with "Gen Eds" (general education requirements), such as English, Biology, World History, or Art. I started my first semester taking those four classes, and I was overwhelmed but I was hooked!

In my second semester, I enjoyed many topics but felt most drawn to those in psychology. I enjoyed speaking with, hearing about, and thinking about people, our thoughts, fears, motivations, behavior, and choices. The only other class that was as interesting to me and felt as mind-blowing, was a class called "Critical Thinking Skills."

Learning About and Developing Critical Thinking Skills

This course was where I got a "real" education on thinking, including concepts like cognitive bias, cognitive dissonance, and other topics under the critical thinking umbrella. For me, having my eyes opened to these concepts in an entire course was a huge gift I absolutely loved. Check it out right now: Do an internet search for "critical thinking cognitive biases" and see what comes up. What do you think about it?

Maybe you've already learned about topics concerning critical thinking, and maybe you haven't. Either way, I truly can't convey all the valuable ways that educating yourself in this area will benefit you. Read and watch videos about it. Consider the endless examples of cognitive dissonance, identify them in your thoughts and in those of other people you meet in life. Please trust me when I say that managing cognitive dissonance and deploying your critical thinking skills will make you smarter, and save you from wasting immeasurable amounts of time, energy, and frustration in your life. As we'd say in the hair and beauty industry, "Work smarter, not harder!"

A year after the critical thinking course, my communication, time management, and study skills had hit a new high. My confidence and determination had never been stronger. I had another client that enjoyed hearing about my college journey, who recommended one four-year private college in particular. It accepted transfer credits from other colleges, and she thought I would enjoy attending. Having gotten to know me, based on our professional relationship and her understanding of my aptitudes, she offered to write me a letter of recommendation.

Though I had a newfound confidence, the idea of a big new challenge like this felt super scary. For some weeks, I hesitated! It was outside my comfort zone, something I had only wondered and fret about. It was the great unknown! But you know what else? Deep down, I knew I had to muster the courage, curiosity, and creativity to succeed. Why? I think it's best said with a portion of another delightful quote. Lewis Carroll wrote: "In the end, we only regret the chances we didn't take..." With that sentiment in my gut and heart, I accepted my client's offer with excitement and gratitude, though I didn't know all the places it would lead me.

Time marched on, and much occurred. I learned how to apply for financial aid, got some Pell Grants, took on some loans, and continued working part-time as a hairstylist – now on my own. I had left the salon world and struck out solo with a handful of clients, by stocking my own supplies and doing their hair in their homes. Then another client gave me a gift, by telling me about exams I could take for knowledge I already possessed. I reviewed the CLEP exam website and decided which exams I wanted to take to earn college credit cheap and fast! I filed this plan away until months later, when I knew I would have more time in my packed schedule for extra studying and the actual exam appointment dates.

I had been scheming about ways to do a semester abroad, and one autumn, I was able to afford it. By renting out the room in my shared apartment to an exchange student, I did a semester abroad in Chengdu. Shortly after I returned, I realized I wanted to make a career transition to a team environment where I could still be creative and social, but learn and grow in different ways. I sought a job as an administrative assistant at a university and landed it. From there my experiences working in universities began.

The Power of Research: Expanding Your Knowledge

With another big life transition and my constant immersion in working and learning, I was becoming a creative problem-solving force to be reckoned with. The most significant skill contributors? (Aside from the powerful three.) Critical thinking and *research*. I was being forced to look for the answers to endless problems, and I was learning that there is an answer for just about everything. Including when there isn't. Because sometimes, the answer is that there is no one right answer. Others times, the answers are out there but the knowledge required to understand the answers is so vast and complex that we may not be able to truly understand it. But that again is a kind of answer. It's as close to an answer as you might get – unless you choose to learn more deeply in which case there's more answers to be found. The bottom line is: you can, and should, come to conclusions about answers only after thinking, and researching, and thinking some more!

And realize, more answers mean conclusions can change. Understand all of this, embrace it, and you'll smash it out there.

Think about it. We live in the "Age of Technology" where information is instantly available – more and more. Previous generations wondered and speculated. They'd say, "I don't know...it's probably X or Y." then launch into whatever answer they were emotionally attached to or was accepted by those around them. Because of this habit, a lot of older folks don't simply say, "Huh, I don't know." without feeling anxious or inadequate. But they also don't become as curious. Younger people do this too, but I'm bringing up the fact that *some* of the older generation do this because they *had* to speculate. Because more often than not, they didn't have a personal computer and the internet on their person at *every waking moment*. They didn't as readily understand and couldn't as easily accept, that if they couldn't know or didn't understand something in their immediate view of the world, that the tried and true answers were still out there, somewhere. That *others do know* and *do understand*. And that with the internet, they could find real answers, if they developed their skills in finding them. So learn this now. Learn to say, "Huh, I don't know." and follow up with "What do you think?" to hear the information and opinions of others. *Then cement your habit* of trying to find more answers and opinions, by using your favorite search engine, *for everything*.

Some people will think this is overkill. But guess what? It's the most powerful way to learn. It's exactly how we learn languages. If you don't know the definition of a word, you look it up in the dictionary. It's the same concept, just a different tool. If you don't know about something, look it up. Read articles, watch videos, and don't shy away from scholarly papers. The answers are there for the taking! Honestly, I can promise you this: If you ask a search engine for every single thing you don't know about, after a few weeks you'll feel your problem-solving abilities soaring. After a few months, your critical thinking skills and confidence may even shock you. You'll feel how much you're improving your quality of life and maybe that of those around you. You're working smarter, not harder! You're creating more opportunities for your ambitions, for your dream life.

Critical Thinking and Research Skills Paying Off

In my third year of college, I made a big effort to carve out more time for studying and exams. I took the CLEP exams on English Literature and Natural Sciences. I paid around $300 and earned six credits, saving myself the money and time I would have spent on two full-semester courses!

It took five years from starting at community college until I graduated from my four-year school. I emerged with cherished friendships, a workplace I loved, some student loan debt, and confidence I could take on the future.

Did I save boatloads of money from working part-time in school, from the hacks I used to get an excellent education, and from getting credit for the knowledge I already had? Yep! Did I struggle like crazy? You bet! Did it all pay off in all kinds of ways? Absolutely.

Beyond my college days, I've held several good jobs, traveled quite a bit, made friends in various parts of the world, taken certification courses for cool new skills, and have made career transitions based on different life callings, to feel fulfilled. I've embraced the skills I use naturally, bulked them up with specialized education, and found my career of choice. I get satisfaction from connecting with others who want a collaborator, resources, tools, inspiration, and problem-solving support. Watching others benefit from growth and happiness brings me great happiness in return.

How did I make such strategic decisions about my time, money, social life, living situations, travel, and have the energy for it all?

Powerful life skills! Personal growth and education aren't just about absorbing knowledge; they're about transforming your mind into a lean, mean-thinking machine. That is how countless people, including myself, have masterminded the achievement of dreams for our lives.

As we bring this chapter to a close, I want to thank you for sharing in my journey. I hope it has become clear why I'm so passionate about this topic and why I want you to gain powerful life skills, take on adulting, and create your own dream life!

Other tips for cultivating your critical thinking skills early on? Embrace diverse perspectives, set goals for improvement, take classes where you'll actively participate, and practice problem-solving. Seek out thought-provoking lectures, engaging discussions, and the occasional late-night philosophical debate with friends. These are mental workouts like no other. Add all of the knowledge, advice, and tools in this book to your toolbelt! And always remember that research and critical thinking are incredible tools for success. (Auld, 2019)

As you gear up for Chapter 2, "Gaining and Maintaining Confidence," get ready to supercharge yourself. Confidence is also critical for success. I will explain why it's so important, how to stay positive, and how to handle roadblocks. Envision yourself exuding unshakable confidence, standing tall in your independence.

You've got this!!

Chapter 2
Gaining and Sustaining Confidence

"You can, you should, and if you're brave enough to start, you will."

-Stephen King

With a firm grasp on self-confidence, its significance, and tips on how to sustain it, you can get the most out of it to tackle issues, craft an individual identity, and accomplish more across all elements of your life.

Confidence isn't just a buzzword; it's a skill and a tool for success. In the ever-changing arena of life, confidence is your shield against doubts and your sword for conquering challenges.

Crafting a Resilient Mindset: A powerful skill for College, Trade School, or Whatever You Decide...and Beyond

Now, picture yourself stepping onto a college, training, or corporate campus, a backpack casually hanging over your shoulder. You realize, it's not just the weight of books and the laptop you're carrying – it's the weight of dreams and ambitions, too. And you know what? You're not the only one. Look around; every other student or co-worker you see carries a similar load of hopes, questions, and the quest to find where they fit in.

Your educational and workplace adventures aren't just about lugging around supplies or rushing from one place to another. They are journeys into a whole new world of knowledge, friendships, and self-discovery. Picture yourself confidently speaking in front of a crowd, diving into the technological pool, leading a team with finesse, or managing conflicts gracefully. These aren't far-fetched dreams; they're the stepping stones of your confidence journey. Picture these scenarios as building blocks of your inner confidence.

Here's the scoop: A staggering 85% of people have grappled with low self-esteem according to Dr. Joe Rubino, a globally recognized authority on self-esteem building, personal development, and success coaching. So, if you've had your moments of self-doubt, welcome to the club!

Still you might wonder, what's the real deal with self-confidence? Is it a rare gift reserved for the elite few, or something you're simply born with?

Know this: Confidence isn't a mystical force reserved for a chosen bunch. It's not a fixed trait; it's born from your thoughts and actions. It's not merely about conquering tasks; it's about believing in your potential. As you sail across lectures, tests, and difficult waves, your inner voice whispers, "You're capable of this."

When you think of it as a muscle, it becomes pretty straightforward – the more you flex it, the stronger it gets.

You control your confidence levels. You can swap uncertainty for courage. It's not set in stone; you can dial it up. Here's the secret: Act as if you're already brimming with confidence. Visualize an inner fire blazing, illuminating every step you take. What's that fire? It's your unwavering belief in your abilities. It's your self-confidence. It's no fleeting emotion; it's a certainty that greatness is within your grasp. Just as a bonfire needs nurturing to burn bright, your self-confidence requires your attention to keep it aflame.

Speak up, stretch, and exit your comfort zone! You're the director of your blockbuster – confidence is your leading star. And when that confidence wavers – as it does for everyone – envision fanning the flames. Recall your victories, big and small. Conquered a daunting assignment? Navigated a nerve-wracking social event? Each accomplishment adds sparks to your self-assuredness, making it shine even brighter.

So, on your journey through high school, college, a training program, and beyond, remember: self-confidence isn't a mere ally; it's your guiding North Star, shining within yourself.

How to regain your self-confidence, even when it dips

Picture your mind as a bustling toolshed, its shelves stocked not with hammers and nails but with thoughts and perspectives. As you venture into life after high school or another experience, imagine yourself as the master craftsperson of this intricate mental landscape.

Now, let's delve into a concept that might make you roll your eyes at first glance: the "positive mindset." You've probably encountered this phrase countless times, and you might be tempted to dismiss it casually: "Yeah, yeah, be positive. Got it." However, hang on for a moment because this goes far beyond just a catchy slogan.

It's easy to brush off the notion as another piece of fluffy self-help advice. However, it's really a potent tool that can shape your experience as you tackle new educational chapters and beyond. But here's the catch: it's not about faking happiness or pretending that life is a never-ending party. Instead, it's about nurturing an outlook that equips you to handle life's full spectrum – the highs, the lows, and the curveballs you never saw coming.

Let's visualize your mindset as a pair of glasses. When you're faced with a challenge, you have two options for lenses – a blurry pair that magnifies the difficulty or a clear, focused set that reveals opportunities within challenges.

Reframing is more than just a simple analogy – it's a powerful mindset hack. Think of it as changing your perspective, like switching to a different pair of glasses that offer you a new view of the world.

Imagine hitting a roadblock in your studies – instead of letting frustration steer the wheel, swap it out for curiosity. Transform the defeated thought of "This is impossible" into the empowering belief of "This is a chance to challenge myself and grow." With this shift, challenges morph into opportunities to hone your problem-solving skills and achieve personal growth. The goal isn't to deny the existence of problems but to pivot your focus from the problem to the solutions that can surmount it. A brilliant term for this skill is "being solution-oriented." It's about being proactive instead of reactive, finding ways to learn and grow from your obstacles.

Reactivity vs. Proactivity: Why your approach matters

Being proactive means becoming a dedicated problem-solver. You can't bury your head in the sand, pretending problems don't exist. That's like ignoring a tornado and hoping it will simply blow over. So instead of throwing your hands up and surrendering with a defeated "Well that's just my luck," roll up your sleeves and inquire, "Alright, how can I tackle this?" With a positive mindset as your ally, every interaction, lecture, and challenge can be approached with an attitude that confidently declares, "I can handle this."

Now, when those inevitable setbacks crop up (and trust me, they're as common as ants at a picnic), your hopefulness will be the very thing to turn them around. I know because I've faced my share of them. And believe me, each one felt like it'd break my resolve to pieces. But I wouldn't give them the power. I held on to hope like a sailor holds on to their ship during a rough storm. During setbacks I'd ask myself, how can I get through this? How can I have courage, be curious, or be creative?

A positive mindset isn't just a whimsical notion; it's grounded in science.

Let me to introduce you to Barbara Fredrickson, a psychology expert hailing from the University of North Carolina. She's spent decades delving into the realm of positive emotions. And her discoveries? They're eye-opening. Individuals who embrace a positive outlook recover faster after stumbling and exhibit greater resilience overall. (Fredrickson, 2023)

Let's envision a positive mindset as fuel for a rocket propelling your potential. The aim isn't to ignore challenges but to gear up with an attitude that boldly declares, "Alright, universe, show me what you've got!"

So, you might wonder, how do we go about having this positive mindset? Let's dive into the nitty-gritty of cultivating this transformative attitude.

Step One: Defeating Your Inner Critic

You know the voice – the one that loves to rain on your parade.

Well, it's time for a transformation. Empower it to become your loudest cheerleader rather than letting it drag you down. When it begins to whisper doubts, silence it with a dose of positivity.

Imagine this: you're tackling an important assignment, and that annoying voice pipes up with, "You'll never finish this on time."

Tell yourself: "I hear you, but you've got this. You've triumphed over challenges before, and you're going to do it again."

Boom! You've put a stop to that thought, and you trek on.

Oh, and here's a magic word: "*yet.*" Incorporate it into your vocabulary, particularly when confronted with new challenges. When your inner critic tries to assert, "I can't handle this," counter with a confident, "I can't handle this... yet." It's like planting a seed of potential that will assist you in navigating rough patches. After all, you've not only survived them but thrived despite them.

Then, search for words and phrases that help you complete the next thought. "I'll be able to handle this..." "...once I've taken a break to gain energy." "...once I complete the reading on this subject." "...once I've talked to my mentor about it and thought about the decision I want to make."

These are powerful tools you can use to guide you on your journey on the unfamiliar paths of life.

Step Two: Embracing Gratitude

Grasping the positive and negative emotions that come with changes is a must-have for getting through the tough times with your feelings and stress levels in check.

Gratitude isn't merely a trend on social media; it's a practice that can genuinely elevate your well-being. It's not about downplaying struggles but recognizing the small victories, moments of connection, and sources of joy. Imagine it as a pocketful of radiant moments you can retrieve when times get tough.

It isn't just some fleeting social media fad – it's a serious superpower for boosting your happiness! And recognizing that both negative and positive emotions can exist side-by-side. Just as yesterday's news doesn't define today's reality, embracing both positive and negative emotions is more than a catchphrase; it's a profound strategy.

So, when maintaining a "positive mindset" surfaces, don't send it back to the deep. Embrace it as a lifeline that boosts your inherent strength.

Common Obstacles to Confidence and Happiness

Let's break down some common obstacles to confidence and happiness and the not-so-secret secrets to overcoming them:

Loneliness:

I experienced a sharp sense of isolation during my first year of college. It was like being the odd one out at a gathering, but it stuck with me. Overcoming loneliness starts by stepping out of your comfort zone. Join clubs, attend social events, and don't be shy about striking up conversations. You'll be surprised how quickly those lonely moments fade into the background!

Living to Please Others:

Living to please others can be downright draining - we're like waiters constantly taking orders, but never getting to taste the meal ourselves.

I used to bend over backward to please everyone, but it left me drained. Overcoming this involves finding your voice. Remember, it's okay to say no, set boundaries, and prioritize your well-being.

Jealousy/Comparing Yourself to Others:

Jealousy is like peeping through the window of your neighbor's house - you might think they're having a party but really, they're probably just doing their laundry. Instead, embrace your journey and celebrate all your successes. If you have the habit of scrolling through social media and envying people's perfect lives, realize it's just a highlight reel, not the entire movie. To overcome jealousy, focus on your journey. Celebrate your victories, no matter how small, and remember, everyone has their struggles behind the scenes.

Over-Competitiveness:

Competition can be healthy, but when it becomes all-consuming, it's a joy-killer. The secret here is to remember that not everything is a competition. Learn to collaborate, not just compete, and you'll find that success tastes sweeter when shared.

Fear of Missing Out (FOMO):

FOMO is like obsessing over that friend who always seems to be at cool parties while you're home watching Netflix or doing self-care. But guess what? You're not missing out on life; you're living it. The secret to overcoming FOMO is to embrace the present moment. Be where you are, and remember that social media often -if not always- paints a misleading picture!

Focus on Physical Things:

We can all fall into the trap of chasing material things like they're the key to happiness. Spoiler alert: they're not. Overcoming this obstacle starts with a shift in perspective. Focus on experiences and relationships. Memories last longer than things and the joy of a good conversation outweighs any fancy gadget.

Self-Absorption:

We all have moments of self-absorption, but it's a happiness thief. The secret to overcoming it is simple: practice empathy. Ask people about their day, listen actively, and you'll find that connecting with others brings a deeper sense of fulfillment.

Victim Mentality:

A victim mentality is like playing the blame game, but you're always the loser - you never take the time to recognize your role in your challenges and setbacks.

Blaming everyone and everything for your problems is exhausting, and it only holds you back. To overcome a victim mentality, take responsibility for your life. Acknowledge that you have the power to change your circumstances and steer your ship towards better waters!

Complaining:

Complaining can be cathartic, but when it's constant, it's like a dark cloud following you around. The secret to breaking this habit is simple: gratitude. Recognize the things in life you have to be grateful for daily, and you'll find less to complain about. Then feel the difference in yourself – feel how much you seem to struggle less!

On the grand journey of life, these obstacles are like potholes on the road—annoying but manageable. The secrets to overcoming them aren't secrets at all; they're about embracing authenticity, empathy, and gratitude. (Falcon, 2015)

This chapter has provided tools and insights for drawing on confidence and navigating challenges to develop your identity. We've explored the significance of self-confidence, the value of a positive attitude, and common obstacles to confidence and strategies for avoiding and overcoming them. In the world of adulting, confidence is the golden ticket. Set your goals high, embrace the challenges, and remember: You're not just here to survive; you're here to thrive.

Let's start this new adventure together. Let's envision a future built on a never-ending courageous spirit. One of experiments, accomplishments, caring connections, and financial acumen that bring our aspirations to fruition. So stay tuned because I'm about to drop some seriously savvy advice to help you rock this adulting gig!

Chapter 3
Managing Pressure and Stress

"Believing you are unworthy of love and belonging -that who you are authentically is a sin or is wrong- is deadly.
Who you are is beautiful and amazing."

-Laverne Cox

I n this chapter, we're going to dive deep into a topic that's all too familiar: managing pressure and stress. Remember that stress is a natural response to many challenges, and in moderation, it can be a motivating force. However, you might have times when it feels too much.

Here you're about to get a quick sneak peek into Chapter 4. Because managing pressure and stress is a form of self-care. And self-care is a form of self-love. Hence the start of this chapter with this brilliant, essential quote by Laverne Cox. Practice the powerful life skills in this book, and employ every other resource and habit you must, to understand that your love for yourself, just as from others, is an essential ingredient for managing pressure and stress, and having a healthy, happy, powerful, life. Period.

Now, if you're feeling so much pressure from others, or from yourself, that you aren't feeling love in your life, you could be in trouble. Pressure and stress should never make you believe that who you are isn't good, isn't enough, or unworthy of love to the point where you don't really feel any. If you're not sure what to do, or you feel you can't manage it, I'm going to tell you what to do right now. You're going to skip ahead a few steps, and seek advice from a professional. Make appointments with one or more until you make a good connection with one who truly understands your feelings, and will make meaningful recommendations that will help you regain the self-love you need to manage stress.

By recognizing pressure and stress in your life and using powerful life skills and strategies, you can problem solve effectively to regain your confidence, inner peace, and ability to thrive. You can continue creating your powerful dream life, which you 100% deserve to do.

Got it, my friend?

Ok, now, buckle up as we stride confidently onward and explore how to manage life's juggling act, handle pressure, and take masterfully good care of ourselves as we keep our eyes firmly fixed on creating your dream life! The next lesson is Healthy Boundaries.

The Importance of Healthy Boundaries & Examples of What They Look Like

Quite often, when you have many challenges and pressures in a particular phase of life, you may find yourself in need of multiple healthy-boundary-setting techniques. Because, with seemingly endless work to complete, social activities, and pressure from parents or guardians, life can often feel like an unending rollercoaster ride. Think of these boundary techniques as trusty safety goggles for your experiments in the world of adulting. The pressures will come and go, and the choices you make to handle them are opportunities to grow powerful.

Let's explore some areas of life you will need to practice setting boundaries around:

Time Management: Setting boundaries around your time is crucial. Establish a study schedule and allocate sufficient time for coursework, while also dedicating time for socializing and self-care. Communicate your schedule to your friends so you don't seem to over-commit to social events and neglect your coursework.

Personal Space: Your personal space is sacred. It's essential to communicate your need for alone time or privacy when necessary. In shared living arrangements, discuss and establish ground rules with roommates to ensure everyone's comfort. Also remember, your approach to personal space shouldn't ignore your roommate's privacy or evade shared living rules.

Academic Priorities: Maintain boundaries concerning your academic priorities. When you're faced with conflicting commitments, such as social events and study sessions, have the discipline to prioritize your studies when needed. (However, consistently prioritizing only one area of your life may not be a healthy boundary, but a red flag for anxiety or other feelings. If you feel yourself struggling with this, reach out to your supportive resources.)

Emotional Well-being: Acknowledge and respect your emotional boundaries. It's okay to set limits on the kind of emotional support you provide to others, especially when you're dealing with your own challenges. Constantly sacrificing your emotional well-being for others isn't a healthy option when you have your challenges to deal with (Pattemore, 2021).

Again, life can be unpredictable and unimaginably challenging. Despite your meticulous planning, there will be times when life throws you a curveball, and you find yourself off track. Maybe you missed a deadline, or had a conflict with someone. Maybe you've been struggling with parental pressures, or your job or your coursework. It's ok - we've all been there. In the next section, there are more powerful life skills to practice that can help you regain your confidence, your healthy mindset, and your ability to focus on what matters.

Dealing with Peer Pressure & How to Communicate Your Priorities to Others

Peer pressure is a subtle yet powerful force that lurks in the background during and after our most intense educational years. It doesn't vanish, but it changes its form. This understanding dawned on me as I navigated my trade school training, paid work and college years, where understanding and managing peer pressure became paramount. (Coping with Peer Pressure, n.d.)

Now picture this scenario: Your friends are urging you to attend a late-night party on the eve of a significant exam. Healthy boundaries would enable you to assertively decline while preserving your friendships. Letting peer pressure override your better judgment will lead to added stress and academic challenges.

I'm not going to lie, it was challenging for me to master this one. But over time I armed myself with prepared responses for scenarios like this, and it got easier. I had a polite but definitive answer: "I appreciate the invite, but I have to pass! See you later!" I also learned to propose alternatives that resonated with my values. When pressured to skip studying, I suggested forming a study group or choosing specific dates and times for hangouts. I didn't lose my social life, and I gained sanity and self-respect!

Effective communication is key to achieving peace with your roommate, project group, or family. As another example, I once had a roommate who loved blasting music. Instead of telling her to stop, I asked her to lower the volume while I needed to study, enough so that I couldn't hear it, or use headphones. We agreed that I would let her know when I planned to study, which helped her understand and expect certain times when she'd need to limit loud music in her room. By being upfront with my needs and determined to negotiate, the effort resulted in our lives being more peaceful. It was a good lesson in effective communication and finding common ground.

Keeping Some Thoughts and Plans Private, Versus Sharing Them

The balance between keeping your thoughts and plans private and sharing them with others can be a nuanced one. It's a bit like knowing when to whisper secrets in the dark versus when to shout your triumphs from the rooftops. You'll often grapple with this decision, whether it's regarding your academic aspirations, personal struggles, or life plans.

Here are a few considerations to help you navigate this delicate balance:

Assessing Trust: Determine the level of trust you have with the person or group you're considering sharing your thoughts or plans with. Trust is the foundation of fruitful communication.

Defining Boundaries: Set clear boundaries for what you're comfortable sharing and what you'd prefer to keep private. Communicate these boundaries to those close to you.

Identifying Support Networks: Recognize the importance of having a support network that you can confide in. Friends, mentors, or counselors can provide valuable guidance and emotional support (Nash et al., 2018).

Here's an example of a student who valued her emotional well-being, and set a boundary while assessing trust in her social circles:

Jennifer, a determined college student, wanted to start a side hustle making artwork and selling it on Etsy. She hesitated to share this with anyone, fearing their reaction might be criticism of her artistic skills. After careful consideration, she decided to confide in just her mentor, and their supportive response helped alleviate her stress. She spent a few months on her side hustle while keeping it between just her mentor and herself. After some success she shared her activities with more people. Mixed reactions of support and indifference made her feel relieved she had kept it private, and more confident in her ability to know when to share parts of her life with others. She also learned who she could continue to seek support and motivation from.

Learning How to Deal with Difficult People

In school or any phase of life, you will run into people who could make life difficult. This could be a strict professor, a difficult roommate, or working with someone on a group project that proves to be hard. Here are strategies for handling these challenging situations:

Active Listening: When faced with a difficult individual, practice active listening. Seek to understand their perspective and concerns before responding. This empathetic approach can defuse tension and lead to more productive conversations.

Setting Clear Expectations: In group projects or shared living spaces, establish clear expectations from the outset. Define roles and responsibilities, deadlines, and communication protocols to minimize potential conflicts.

Conflict Resolution Skills: Practice conflict resolution techniques such as compromise, collaboration, and assertive communication. These skills can be invaluable when dealing with challenging individuals who might have conflicting interests.

Maintaining Emotional Detachment: Don't let challenging people's emotions dictate your reactions. Maintain emotional detachment, focusing on your goals and objectives (MD & Orloff, 2015).

Here's an example of a student who grappled with difficult individuals on a group project:

David found himself in a group project with a member who consistently resisted collaboration. David managed to understand his teammate's concerns by actively listening to their problems and showcasing assertiveness to find common ground, ultimately gaining the member's trust and respect, leading to a more productive partnership.

Now a different challenge often faced by students, is the burden of parental expectations and academic pressures. Let's figure out how to tackle these pressures and make sure your educational experiences are still awesome.

Handling Parental or Guardian Pressure in Academics

It's common for parents, guardians, and other relatives to have high hopes and expectations for their children's academic success. While their intentions may be well-meaning, these pressures can sometimes become overwhelming. Here's how to manage these expectations while maintaining your own well-being and academic performance:

Open Communication: An open and honest conversation with your parents is the first step. Share your academic goals, challenges, and any stress you may be experiencing. Explain that their support, rather than pressure, will help you excel.

Set Realistic Expectations: Discuss and establish realistic academic goals. While striving for excellence is admirable, it's crucial to avoid setting unattainable standards that lead to stress and burnout. (How to deal with pressure from your parents, 2023)

Highlight Your Achievements: Share your achievements, whether they're big or small. When parents see your progress and dedication, they may find it easier to become more understanding and less pushy.

I recall feeling immense parental pressure during my undergraduate years. My parents, wanting the best for me, would ask me for updates on my coursework every time we spoke, but this increased my anxiety. I planned a meeting with them to discuss my goals and progress to show them I was committed to studying. I also expressed the feelings of stress I experienced but let them know I was managing it in the best way for me. I explained that through my strategies, I was on the path I meant to be on, and the addition of unfounded concern from them was just an added stressor. Their side of the story was that they were just trying to help. I let them know my preferred way they help me: To change their habit of sharing their concerns and offer excitement for my progress, encouragement, and to help me celebrate my successes.

Pro tip: Telling them the best way to help you can be the most important part. Why? Because you are asking for what you need. By doing so, you are actually setting a boundary. If they cross it, you can always refer back to this conversation, where you expressed a preference for a certain type of support. The greatest benefit here is not only their behavior change. It's also feeling strong and secure in having made a clear and reasonable request for their support of you. (Can you say "powerful life skills" three times fast?)

A Guide to Emotion Regulation, Mindset, and Confidence

To get a leg up on managing pressure, we can also learn from the process model of emotion regulation, which comprises five key elements:

1. **Situation Selection:** Choose environments and situations that align with your goals and values. This proactive step helps you avoid unnecessary stressors and pressures.

2. **Situation Modification:** Take control of your surround-

ings by modifying them to reduce stress. Rearrange your workspace, manage your time efficiently, and you're creating circumstances conducive to productivity.

3. **Attention Deployment:** Shift your focus away from stressors and toward positive aspects. Redirect your attention to what you can control, such as your actions and responses.

4. **Cognitive Change:** Challenge negative thought patterns and replace them with positive and constructive thinking. This change in mindset can significantly impact how you perceive and manage pressure.

5. **Response Modification:** Adjust your emotional and behavioral responses to pressure. Practice relaxation techniques, deep breathing, and stress-reduction exercises to maintain composure. (Psych Central, 2022)

Prioritizing and Balancing Your Responsibilities

One of the biggest pressure points in a new program or job is juggling your priorities. Learning the balancing act has a boatload of benefits. It's not just about avoiding burnout (although that's a pretty huge win). It's also about boosting your success in both your academic and personal life. You've got classes, maybe a job, extracurricular activities, and a social life.

I remember when trying to keep up with all these things felt like I was walking a tightrope. But when I got the hang of it, life became a whole lot more enjoyable. Remember, it's always important to maintain your equilibrium while juggling the many demands of your new-and-different-looking life.

Understanding Your Priorities: Urgent vs. Important

Understanding the difference between urgent and important tasks can significantly enhance your ability to manage pressure and make informed decisions.

Urgent Tasks: Urgent tasks demand immediate attention due to impending deadlines or a time-sensitive nature. Examples include:

- Submitting assignments or papers before the deadline.

- Studying for an exam scheduled for the next day.

- Responding to urgent emails from bosses, professors or team members.

Important Tasks: Important tasks contribute to your long-term goals and well-being. They may not have immediate deadlines but are crucial for your overall success. Examples include:

- Long-term project planning and research.

- Investing time in building meaningful relationships with professors, bosses, colleagues or mentors.

- Taking care of your physical and mental health through regular exercise and self-care routines (Greene, 2023).

Let's visualize a scenario, then check out 10 powerful skills and habits to understand the options we have for maintaining that work-life balance.

Imagine this: It's the week before finals, and you're overwhelmed by a tidal wave of study guides, term papers, and group projects. The mounting pressure makes you wonder if you'll ever see the light at the end of the tunnel.

1. **Get Organized**: Organization is your best friend. Use planners, apps, or whatever suits your style to keep track of deadlines and commitments. Trust me; it's a game-changer.

2. **Communicate with Family, Friends, and Employers**: Let your loved ones and your boss know about your commitments and schedule. Clear communication can help prevent unnecessary stress.

3. **Maintain a Healthy Lifestyle**: Eating well, getting enough sleep, and staying active might sound basic, but they're your secret weapons for keeping your energy levels up.

4. **Practice Mindfulness**: Take a breather and practice mindfulness techniques like meditation or yoga. They can work wonders in reducing stress.

5. **Devote Time to Hobbies**: Don't forget to make time for the things you love. Hobbies are like little joy factories that can keep you motivated. (The Balancing Act, 2018)

6. **Set Limits**: Learn to say no whenever necessary to aid your responsibilities or well-being. Overcommitment can lead to overwhelm, and nobody wants that. Don't live to please.

7. **Lower Your Expectations**: Perfectionism can be your enemy. Strive for excellence, but remember that you're human.

8. **Take Breaks**: Regular breaks during study or work sessions

boost productivity. It's science! Just be sure it's a *real* break; *real* rest or change of pace. Breaks can turn into procrastination. Learn the difference and you're ahead of the game!

9. **Don't Procrastinate**: Procrastination can be a sneaky time thief. Fight it off with the time management techniques in this list. Try out everything in this book and more, and find out what works best for you!

10. **Ask for Help**: You don't have to do it all alone. Reach out for help when you need it, whether it's from professors, peers, or counselors. (How to Balance Life, Work, and School, n.d.)

Now it's time for the ***Chapter 3 Worksheet***, where you get to build those muscles for managing pressure, boost your self-confidence and practice self-care! After you've completed it, meet me back here and we'll continue onward!

In our journey so far, we've delved into some powerful life skills. On our way to develop our skills for managing pressure, we've discussed the influence of peer and parental pressures, the importance of boundaries, the secrets to balancing priorities, and the significance of deciding what to keep private and what to share.

As we venture into Chapter 4, "Self-Care is Self-Love" we'll delve into the art of handling stress through self-care, and reinforcing the importance of maintaining a healthy mindset in creating your dream life.

Chapter 4
Self-Care Is Self-Love

"Letting go gives us freedom, and freedom is the only condition for happiness. If, in our heart, we still cling to anything -anger, anxiety, or possessions- we cannot be free."

-Thích Nhất Hạnh

Thich Nhat Hanh couldn't be more right. I invite you to consider his quote throughout this chapter, as you experiment with a variety of stress-busting techniques. Because on the journey ahead, you can expect some moments when you feel like you're running a marathon while juggling flaming torches and jumping rope at the same time.

Stress can creep in, set up shop, and before you know it, you're dealing with headaches, acne (yikes!), muscle tension, and the looming threat of heart and autoimmune diseases. Not exactly the transformative experience you signed up for, right?

I remember this part of my college days like they were yesterday – the stress was practically a permanent resident in my life. Ugh, that tension in my neck and shoulders! It was like my body had gone on strike against relaxation, and the ominous shadow of potential health issues lurked in the background. It's safe to say these symptoms weren't part of the rewarding outcomes I had envisioned.

I was drowning in assignments, exams, and pressure. My friend invited me to join a hiking trip, and at first I balked at the idea of taking time away from my studies. But, I could almost feel my body telling me, "I'm under attack! This stress is not going to let your mind refocus until you move around, change your scenery, do breathe deeply and feel refreshed!" Though reluctantly, I agreed to go hiking.

I was surrounded by nature, and the fresh air helped me relax and breathe easier. It was like hitting the reset button on my stress levels. During that hike I realized something crucial. Self-care is self-love. It isn't just a luxury; it's a necessity. You can't be your best self for your studies, your friends, or your future if you're running on empty.

Consider this chapter on ways to handle stress just one of many more incredible resources you can learn from, because it's no secret that we all need a variety of tools and practice to deal with it success-fully. Stressors come in all shapes and sizes, from looming deadlines and heavy workloads to personal conflicts and financial woes. Life's smorgasbord of stressors can leave anyone feeling like they've stepped into the lion's den. But fret not, because stress is a beast that can be tamed.

Now, let's talk about what happens to your body when stress becomes a long-term lodger. It's not a pleasant picture, but knowledge is power, my friends. Following are some physical manifestations of stress:

Effects of Stress on Your Body, Mood, and Behavior

Headaches: Ever feel like a tiny construction worker is hammering away inside your skull? That's the classic stress-induced headache. Long-term stress can turn this occasional nuisance into a frequent companion.

Allergies: Stress can unleash havoc on your immune system, making those allergies you thought you had under control suddenly come roaring back like a vengeful ghost.

Acne: If you thought you left acne back in your teenage years, think again. Stress can trigger breakouts, turning your skin into a battleground of blemishes.

Muscle Tension: Do your shoulders feel like they're slowly migrating toward your ears? Blame stress-induced muscle tension. It's like your body's way of telling you to take a chill pill – literally.

Risk of Cardiovascular Disease and Hypertension: Stress isn't just a mental battle; it's a physical one too. Prolonged stress can increase your risk of cardiovascular diseases and hypertension, putting your heart health on the line.

Anxiety – It's like that jittery feeling before a big exam or a job interview. Your heart races, your palms get sweaty, and you're convinced you'll forget everything you've ever learned. But remember, it's just your brain's way of preparing you. Take deep breaths, sip chamomile tea...choose your own preferred tools and remedies! Whatever you do, tell yourself, "I've got this!"

Restlessness – Ever felt like you can't sit still? Stress can make you feel like you're constantly on the move, like a squirrel searching for its hidden acorns. It's your body's way of saying, "Let's tackle this!" But sometimes, all you need is to lift some weights, a short walk, or some gentle stretching to calm those nerves.

Lack of Motivation/Focus – Assignments piling up like disturbing dishes in the kitchen sink? Stress can make focusing feel like trying to catch smoke with your bare hands. But you can break assignments down into smaller tasks, set goals, and reward yourself when you hit them (like social time or your favorite tv show).

Feeling Overwhelmed – School and jobs can feel like being thrown into a pool without any lessons. When you're overwhelmed with coursework, take a step back and make a to-do list. Ask for help when you need it.

Irritability/Anger – Ever snapped at someone for no apparent reason? Stress can turn you into the Hulk of emotions. Take a breather, go for a run, or punch a pillow (not a person!) to release that tension.

Overeating/Undereating – Stress has a way of messing with your appetite. You might devour a whole pizza or forget to eat for hours. Try to maintain a balanced diet, and don't beat yourself up for the occasional indulgence.

Angry Outbursts – Ever had a mini explosion over something minor? Stress can turn you into a volcano ready to erupt. Find healthy ways to let off steam – like a boxing class or journaling.

Drug or Alcohol Misuse – "Escaping" with substances might seem tempting, but it's a slippery slope. Opt for healthier outlets like joining a club, playing a sport, or belting out your favorite tunes in a karaoke session.

Tobacco Use – Stress might tempt you to light up, but it's like inviting a sneaky gremlin into your life. Instead, take a deep breath of fresh air or try meditation to relax.

The situation may seem bleak, but you've got this! Let's be real – There will be times when you feel like you're in over your head. It's okay. Stress is part of the package deal. It's that unwelcome guest that can mess with your mood, behavior, and overall well-being. But, worry not, because I'm here to help you ride this wave with style and grace.

Here's the thing: It's perfectly normal to feel anxious about the unknowns in life - temporarily. But stress is when those unsavory effects come without warning - and stay too long. When stress and its effects become daily visitors, especially about the same old familiar things, that's when we need to kick it to the curb.

Stress may be part of the journey, but it doesn't define you. It's just another class in the school of life. Armed with the right tools and strategies, your dedication to self-care and a dash of resilience, you can learn how to overcome stress much quicker, with practice.

Adulting Stress Management Techniques

The simplest trick to help you overcome stressful problems? Become calm.

Picture this: You're prepping for a big math exam. Your calculator breaks. You take the metro to a friend's house to borrow hers and on the way there, you accidentally leave your bag with your math book on the train. It's lost forever. Anger, fear and anxiety swoop in like a hurricane. Your heart races, your mind goes blank, and you're convinced you'll fail spectacularly. Been there? We all have. Let's brainstorm some options, in no particular order:

- **A.** Fall to your knees and shout "WHYYYYYYYY!!!" into the heavens.

- **B.** Give up and play hooky on the day of the exam.

- **C.** Contact your school library and ask if they or another nearby library have a copy you can borrow.

- **D.** Find the book online and buy the ebook version to study with.

- **E.** Contact other students in your class to find out if you can borrow theirs or study along with them.

- **F.** Contact your professor and tell them what happened. Ask if they can lend you a copy or tell you where you can get one fast.

- **G.** Based on the book title, find a similar book that contains the same concepts you can study. Buy and download or borrow from the library.

Turns out, you may get to study the material for your exam after all! But before making this list, what is the first thing you need to do when that stress hits? Become calm.

But how???

Temporarily cut off excess stimuli. Even if you're on a bustling city street, you can do this, with practice, I promise. Focus inside yourself. Take several deep breaths. Close your eyes if you need to. Know inside that accidents happen, life happens, that you're determined to find a solution, and that you *WILL*. Only then, make your list of options like I did above. Then try each one, from that place of calm. When stress and those emotions inevitably bubble up again, use your calming techniques - as many times as you need to, until you find the solution or have exhausted every option. Take your time. It might seem counterintuitive, but rushing through any problem makes it much more likely to make mistakes and prolong your time fixing it. Coming from a place of calm may seem like you're wasting time, but it's actually how you're going to come to the best solution - faster than by rushing.

Coping with and Reducing Stress - Because Chill is the New Cool

Imagine this: You're running on three hours of sleep, coffee is your lifeline, and you've forgotten what a weekend feels like. Sound familiar? This is where self-care steps in like a superhero, wearing a cape woven with "me time" and "chill vibes." Now, let's break down the types of self-care:

Basic Self-Care: This is the foundation. It's like brushing your teeth but for your mental well-being. Basic hygiene, eating well, and getting enough sleep fall into this category. You'd be surprised how much a good night's sleep can transform your mood!

Emotional Self-Care: Your emotions are the star of the show here. Express yourself, talk about your feelings, and let it all out. Whether it's through journaling, talking to a friend, or belting out Adele's latest hit in the shower, it's all about processing those emotions.

Physical Self-Care: This is like giving your body a spa day. Exercise regularly, eat nourishing foods, and get enough rest. And don't forget to stay hydrated – it's like giving your body a big, refreshing hug (Psych Central, 2013).

Suggested Self-Care Techniques: Your Stress-Busting Arsenal

College, trade school and jobs can feel like unfamiliar terrain, and managing our stress from a place of uncertain footing can feel treacherous. We need solid techniques to dissolve stress and climb our way back to the path leading to beautiful vistas.

Self-care rituals are habits you develop to make time for yourself. Whether it's taking a walk, meditating, reading for pleasure, or spending time with friends, prioritize activities that rejuvenate your soul. Let's explore 16 practical and manageable ways to create some, all while keeping it real:

1. **Meditation and Mindfulness**: You don't have to be a zen master; a few minutes a day can make a big difference. Apps like Calm and Headspace can guide you.

2. **Journal Whatever Whenever**: Writing down your thoughts and feelings can be incredibly therapeutic. It's like a mental declutter.

3. **Sweat It Out:** Exercise isn't just about those gains. It's also a stress-buster like no other. Whether you hit the gym, join a dance class, or simply take a walk in the park, moving your body is a mood booster. Find out what aerobic activities get your heart pumping and your worries melting away.

4. **Eat Tasty Healthy Foods**: While pizza and ramen are common staples and it's actually a great health hack to indulge in your favorite treat now and then – balance is key! Stand firm in your commitment to fuel your body with nutritious

foods.

5. **Health Literacy:** Knowledge is power. Learn about your body and mind to make informed decisions about your health.

6. **Experience a Digital Detox**: Unplug from screens for a while. It's like giving your brain a mini vacation.

7. **Connect with Your Connections**: Don't be afraid to reach out to friends, family or a mentor when stress gets the better of you. Spend quality time with friends and loved ones. Laughter is the best stress-buster!

8. **Spend Time in Nature**: Take a break in the great outdoors. Fresh air and greenery can work wonders.

9. **Hobbies and Interests (aka Brilliant Stress-Busters)**: Whether it's painting, playing a musical instrument, or cooking, engage in activities that bring you joy.

10. **Sleep Hygiene**: Create a sleep-friendly environment and stick to a consistent sleep schedule. Late-night Netflix binges can be tempting, but prioritize quality sleep for a refreshed mind and body.

11. **The Power of 'No' – Because Boundaries Aren't Just for Chapter 3:** Don't overcommit. It's tempting to join every club, attend every party, and say 'yes' to every favor. But, remember those boundaries we talked about? They apply here too. (Broderick, 2014)

12. **Substance Awareness:** Parties can be fun, but it's essential

to understand the risks of substance misuse and practice moderation.

13. **Sexual Health:** Always prioritize safety and well-being in your relationships.

14. **Reward Yourself:** After a grueling exam or assignment, treat yourself to something special. You've earned it.

15. **Useful Apps:** In this digital age, there's an app for nearly everything. Explore apps like MyFitnessTracker, Calm, Hiking Trail Maps to support your health journey.

16. **Seek Help from a Professional**: If stress becomes overwhelming, don't hesitate to seek support from a counselor or therapist. It's a sign of strength, not weakness (Scott, 2020).

Making Time for Self-Care

Understand that we need to think of and approach self-care like we do eating healthy meals, laundry and grocery shopping. There is no end to spending time daily and weekly on these activities, throughout our entire lives! Sure, there is a start and end to the micro-moments each time we're engaged in them, but the work is never done. A few hours, days or weeks later, we'll be doing them again, without fail.

New to making self-care a high-priority, consistent activity in your life? Struggling with finding the time? Here's a little secret: You don't find time; you make time. Here are 4 more tips to start practicing so you can start building those self-care consistency muscles:

Prioritize Self-Care: Make it non-negotiable. Whether it's a daily meditation, a weekly bubble bath, or monthly outings with friends, mark it on your calendar as if your life depends on it—because it does.

Set Boundaries: Notice how this one keeps popping up? Just like in a relationship, it's okay to say no. Let people know when you need time for yourself, and don't feel guilty about it. Your mental and emotional health is worth protecting.

Start Small: Self-care doesn't have to be a grand production. It can be as simple as a 15-minute walk, journaling your thoughts, or indulging in your favorite snack. It's about what makes you feel good.

Find Your Zen Zone: Discover places on or off-campus where you can unwind. A cozy corner in the library, a park, or a quiet room can become your sanctuary (University of Massachusetts Global [UMG], 2020).

As you advance into new and different educational experiences, it won't take long to recognize that managing your time wisely is the key to achieving success. The ability to effectively allocate your time to coursework, social activities, and personal commitments is that powerful life-changer. In this section, we'll explore essential tools and strategies that will help you master the art of time management:

Habit Stacking

Remember in Chapter 1 when we talked about research skills? Here's another opportunity for you to use them. Habit stacking has been around for ages, but this term for this behavior was coined more recently and it's stolen the heart of productivity lovers the world over. Run that internet search and ask yourself, "In what ways am I already habit stacking? What else do I want to accomplish?" When it's time, do the activity in the worksheet for this chapter – Get journaling, stacking, and practicing.

Weekly/Monthly Planners

One of the timeless classics in the world of time management is the trusty paper planner. Weekly and monthly planners offer a bird's-eye view of your schedule, allowing you to plan, set goals, and track your progress. Here's how to make the most of paper planners:

Regular Updates: Dedicate time each week to update your planner. Note down your class schedules, assignment due dates, and any social or extracurricular commitments.

Prioritize Tasks: Use color coding or symbols to prioritize tasks. Highlight important deadlines and set realistic goals for the week or month.

Break Down Goals: Divide larger assignments or projects into smaller, manageable tasks. This not only helps you stay organized but also prevents overwhelm.

Review and Reflect: At the end of each week or month, take a moment to review your accomplishments and areas for improvement. Adjust your strategies accordingly (Greenwood, 2023).

Calendar Apps

In the digital age, calendar apps have become indispensable tools for time management. They provide flexibility and accessibility, allowing you to access your schedule from various devices and receive reminders for upcoming events and deadlines. Here's how you can maximize the benefits of calendar apps:

Sync Across Devices: Ensure your calendar app is synchronized across all your devices, be it your smartphone, tablet, or laptop. This ensures you're always in the loop.

Color Coding: Similar to paper planners, use color coding to distinguish between different types of events and commitments. For instance, use one color for classes, another for study sessions, and another for social events.

Set Reminders: Make good use of reminders and alerts. Set notifications for important deadlines, meetings, and events to help you stay on top of your schedule.

Block Time for Focus: Allocate specific blocks of time for focused study or work. Calendar apps are excellent for scheduling study sessions, allowing you to allocate dedicated time for each subject (Bobby Rae, 2023).

A paper planner or digital apps and tools both have benefits, so try to find the right combination that works for you.

Organizational Tools

Beyond planners and calendars, digital organizational tools can be your secret weapons for time management. Tools like Evernote, Trello, and Google Suite offer features that help you streamline tasks and collaborate efficiently. Here's how to leverage these organizational tools:

Note-Taking and Organization: Evernote is a powerhouse for note-taking and organizing your study materials. Create notebooks for each subject, store research, and easily search for information.

Task Boards: Trello is an excellent tool for managing tasks and projects. Create boards for different aspects of your life, such as coursework, personal projects, or extracurricular activities. Use cards to break down tasks and track progress.

Collaboration and Productivity: Google Suite tools like Google Docs, Sheets, and Slides facilitate collaboration with peers. Create shared documents for group projects, and enjoy real-time editing and commenting. Flash drives are still a fantastic option for storing and sharing files locally. WeTransfer is a game changer for sharing files. Loom is a delightfully welcome platform for making and sending short videos to others via a simple link.

Cloud Storage: Take advantage of cloud storage offered by these tools to ensure your documents are accessible from anywhere, anytime (Revolution Learning and Development Ltd., 2021).

Now it's time for the ***Chapter 4 Worksheet***, where you get to try out habit stacking for a positive mindset!

To sum up, now that you are aware of the importance of incorporating self-care into your lifestyle, let's review the topics discussed in this chapter.

Stress is a real deal, and it can mess with your mood, behavior, and overall life experience. But guess what? You now understand that self-care is self-love, and therefore extremely important and beneficial. Not only that, but you've got a toolbox full of stress-busting techniques, from physical activities to mindfulness practices and self-care methods.

For the next chapter "Keeping Your Mind & Body Healthy," we'll dive into the world of mind and body, and show you how to navigate life with a healthy lifestyle. Just like managing stress, a multitude of activities to care for your mental and physical health can be relaxing, fun, and rewarding too.

Chapter 5
Keeping Your Mind and Body Healthy

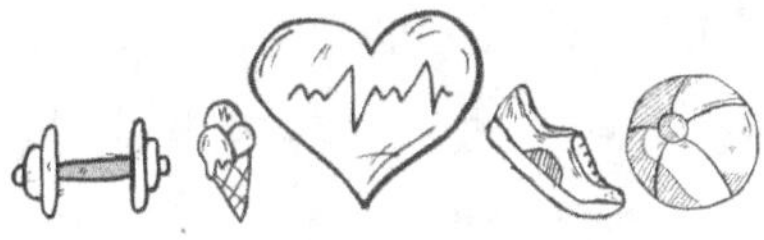

"Take care of your body.
It's the only place you have to live."

-Jim Rohn

As Jim Rohn wisely reminds us, your body is your lifelong residence, and in this chapter, I'll guide you on how to ensure it remains in its best shape. We're about to plunge into a delightful world of health knowledge and tools to put your powerful life skills to work. Review and consider all of your options for nurturing a healthy body and mind throughout life's adventures. Pick your favorites and adopt them as habits.

Keep in mind, there's a million tools, skills, and habits to choose from and they're totally flexible! You can mix and match tools and habits just as much as you want. If something's working for you and anyone tells you, "You're doing it wrong." *They're* doing it wrong! (If you realize you *are* doing it wrong, shrug it off and do it right.) This is your *dream life* you're creating!

Transitioning into a new chapter in life is exciting, but it can also be a period filled with unique challenges. The newfound freedom to experiment with social norms, juggle academics or work, and maintain a healthy work-life balance can be daunting. The stress of more responsibilities can exacerbate existing mental health conditions, such as anxiety and depression, or even trigger new ones. It's essential to be aware of these challenges and their potential impact on your well-being. Let's check out some aspects of health you may not think about much but should develop your skills to focus on. After reading about some of those nasty effects of stress and poor health in the last chapter, you had to know this was coming!

Prioritize Mental Health

The varying demands of life can sometimes feel overwhelming. Social pressures, stress, or a fear of not measuring up can lead to mental strain. Sleep, a precious resource during hectic times, can feel elusive. But remember, you're not alone in this journey. Everyone faces the same or similar challenges. It's crucial to acknowledge and address the potential toll on your mental well-being.

Self-Care for a Balanced Life

You guessed it- Self-care is once again the "secret" to navigating these challenges. We've learned self-care is so much more than pampering yourself; it's about setting aside time for your mental and physical health. Refer to all the brilliant tips and techniques in Chapter 4, for life!

Leveraging An Understanding of Nutrition Will Make You Smarter

You might wonder, "How can what I eat make me smarter?" Well, the food you put in your body has a direct impact on your brain function. Eating right can boost your focus, memory, and overall cognitive abilities. It's like filling the tank of a high-performance car with a superior fuel, to get superior-performance results.

Brain-Boosting Foods

Imagine this: you're prepping for an important exam, and you want your brain firing on all cylinders. What's in your belly and running through your veins, arteries, and organs matters. Think of foods like fish, nuts, berries, and even dark chocolate as your study buddies in food form. They're packed with nutrients that are like superior-performance fuel for your brain. Try them all out!

Finding Out How YOU Stay Healthy

But hold on, there's more. These young adult years are also a great time to figure out your dietary quirks and preferences. Maybe you're lactose intolerant, allergic or sensitive to gluten, vegan, or vegetarian? Knowing these things now can save you from some not-so-fun surprises later. So, get in the habit of paying attention to how your body reacts to different foods. Take note and adjust your food choices accordingly!

Speaking of habits, let's not forget snacking. We all do it, because it's normal and important. But instead of reaching for fatty and sugary things like fried potato chips or candy bars, try healthier options like regular or vegan yogurt, fresh fruit, whole grain or vegan crackers, regular or vegan cheese, lean proteins, nut butters, smoothies, chips and salsa, veggies and hummus, nuts and berries... Need I go on?

Healthy in College: Meal Planning 101

I know. School and work can be crazy busy, and those late-night pizza runs can be hard to resist. But let me share with you based on my own experience: Eating healthy even when you're busy or stressed doesn't have to be a drag. It's all about making some simple changes to your routine. Let's talk about meal planning. Yeah, I know it might sound boring or frustrating, but trust me, it's a game-changer. Plus, you've got this!

Establish the habit of allocating time on a Sunday (or any day that suits you) to plan your meals for the week. It doesn't have to be fancy - even basic dishes can be tasty, nutritious and will even make you feel better and happier!

Imagine this: You've just had a crazy day of work; lectures, assignments, and maybe even time at a job. The last thing you want to do is spend hours in the kitchen. That's where meal planning swoops in to save the day. You open the fridge and find the exact ingredients you bought to make a simple, fast and delicious healthy meal in under 15 minutes. As you assemble the ingredients you begin to feel your feelings of irritability and frustration subside. As you eat your meal or snack, your belly is filled and the feeling of hunger begins to leave you, you become overwhelmed with gratitude for your foresight and wisdom. It's a beautiful thing. If that isn't powerful my friends, well, quite honestly, I don't know what is.

So, look at 5 practical tips to make meal planning a walk in the park. (Or perhaps, a walk of the grocery store aisles and the span of your kitchen):

Use What You Have: Before you start, take a look at what's in your pantry, fridge, and freezer. You'll be surprised at how many meal ideas you can come up with using what you already have.

Plan it Out: Get yourself a meal planning worksheet. It might sound old-school, but writing things down helps. List out your meals for the week, including breakfast, lunch, dinner, and snacks.

Embrace the Delicious: Write a list of healthy foods and recipes you enjoy. No need to turn into a gourmet chef here. Stick to dishes you love, and you're more likely to stick to your plan.

Leftovers are Gold: Don't underestimate the power of leftovers. Cook a bit more than you need, and you'll have a meal ready for the next day. It's like a gift from past you to future you.

Schedule It: Look at your weekly schedule. Do you have a heavy class day on Wednesdays? Plan for something quick and easy. On the flip side, if you have more free time on weekends, then those are your days for shopping and cooking larger portions to have leftovers for the week. If you have a real love for cooking, maybe you even want to whip up something fancy! (Maryville University, 2019)

Healthy Meals for Busy Young Adults - A Sample Meal Plan

What does a meal plan look like? It's just a series of lists! Try this out. Heck, try it right now!

1. Make separate lists of your favorite foods, favorite snack combos, and favorite meals.

2. When you're ready to try meal planning, choose the foods

you want to eat for the week. List them out.

3. Plug those foods into a list: 7 days of 3 meals a day, plus snacks

4. Make a shopping list. (Consider how much you'll need to cover the week.)

Aaand...Go!

Still feeling uninspired? Don't worry, I've got you covered. Check out the meal plan below. The foods I suggest are to give you an idea of how to get energy and nutrients into your body throughout the day. The types of energy and nutrients you choose is up to you!

Also, you'll notice that this meal plan doesn't have a the highest possible repetition of ingredients, which means you'd need to have more of fresh foods handy and cook more often. Some of you may prefer to go this route and more power to you! But what I'm suggesting, at least to start with, is to go for the technique I explained above; do one shopping trip and use the same ingredients throughout the week in different ways. Get the idea? This is another great place to practice your research skills. Some food bloggers focus on this art! Check out their meal plans for using ingredients in creative ways. Hey, if you enjoy the creative problem-solving of meal planning too, maybe you'll want to start a food blog of your own!

Day 1:
Breakfast: Scrambled Eggs with Spinach & Cheese
Lunch: Turkey & Avocado Wrap with a Side Salad
Snack: Yogurt with Honey & Berries
Dinner: Baked Salmon with Roasted Vegetables & Quinoa

Day 2:

Breakfast: Overnight Oats with Chia Seeds & Almond Butter

Lunch: Quinoa Salad with Beets, Cucumbers, & Citrus Dressing

Snack: Veggie sticks & pita chips with Hummus

Dinner: Stir-fried tofu with Mixed Veggies & Brown Rice

Day 3:

Breakfast: Banana, Peanut Butter & Soymilk Smoothie

Lunch: Spinach & Cheese Stuffed Chicken Breast with Brown Rice

Snack: Apple Slices with Almonds

Dinner: Whole Wheat Pasta with Pesto, Olives & Cherry Tomatoes

Day 4:

Breakfast: Yogurt Parfait with Granola & Mixed Berries

Lunch: Grilled Cheese Sandwich with Tomato Soup

Snack: Trail Mix (Nuts and Dried Fruits) & a Banana

Dinner: Meat lovers (or Vegan meat lovers) or Veggie Pizza

Day 5:

Breakfast: Breakfast Burrito with Eggs, Black Beans & Salsa

Lunch: Greek salad with Greek Dressing

Snack: Sliced Cucumber with Tzatziki Sauce

Dinner: Chicken or Black Bean Tacos with Avocado & Salsa

Don't forget to stay hydrated throughout the day with plenty of water, and you can always adjust portion sizes to meet your appetite. Happy meal planning! (Fitness & Nutrition In College, 2023)

Types of Exercise to Choose From - To Keep You Coming Back

Now, you might be wondering, "What kind of exercise can I do that I won't hate?" Well, my friend, you've got options.

I've had the same problem during different phases of life. Sometimes I tried to exercise regularly, but I didn't want to do cardio like jogging or running. But knowing how much it helped my energy and health, I tried things until I found out I preferred climbing stairs. Boom! I went up and down stairs in the comfort of my own home, and also used a stairmaster at my school gym. Don't fret if it takes a bit of trial and error to find the exercise that suits you best. It's all part of the journey to a healthier, happier you.

Now, there are three main types of exercises that you can choose from, or even combine, to create the perfect workout for you:

Aerobic Exercise: This one's all about getting your heart pumping. Think brisk walking, jogging, cycling, or even dancing to your favorite tunes! It's not just great for your cardiovascular health; it's a fantastic stress-buster too. So, if you've got some pent-up frustrations from that tough exam, put on your sneakers and go for a run (or climb stairs)!

Anaerobic Exercise: Now, this is where you can channel your inner superhero. Anaerobic exercises are all about short bursts of intense activity. We're talking about things like sprinting, weightlifting, or high-intensity interval training (HIIT). These workouts can help you build strength and endurance. Not only that - did you know that muscle health contributes to bone health?

Flexibility Exercise: Don't forget to keep those muscles, ligaments and tendons limber to reduce stress on well, everything. Flexibility exercises include yoga, Pilates, or just simple stretching. They're perfect for winding down after a long day of classes and can help prevent those dreaded muscle cramps during late-night study sessions. (Types Of Exercise, 2019)

Workout Options At Your Fingertips

Let's address the elephant in the room - gym memberships can be pricey, and as a student, budgeting is a real thing. But guess what? There are plenty of ways you can stay active without breaking the bank.

First off, check out your campus resources. Many school and workplaces have fitness centers that offer discounted or even free access to students and employees. My college gym had decent equipment, and the best part was I could hit the treadmill or lift weights without worrying about extra expenses. It's a great way to stay in shape without burning a hole in your wallet.

Next up, consider enjoying the great outdoors. Nature's your gym, my friend. Whether it's hiking, biking, or just taking a stroll in the park, getting outside not only gets you moving but also provides a much-needed break from those textbooks, and offers that sense of well-being that only nature can.

At-Home Workouts

Let's talk about something that's often overlooked but brilliant for your well-being. Have you considered or tried home workouts? You don't need fancy equipment to break a sweat. There are tons of apps and online videos that guide you through workouts you can do right in your dorm room. All you need is a yoga mat, a little space, and some determination. Whether you're a student, employee, or someone juggling multiple roles, at-home workouts can be your secret weapon for staying fit and focused. Give it a try!

Easy Study Break Exercises

Now, let's be real. School or work life often means long hours glued to your computer screen, and that can take a toll on your body. The solution? Quick and easy exercises that give your studying muscles a break. Here's a little trick that I learned from somebody at one of my full-time jobs: Every twenty minutes, look away from your screen twenty feet away, for at least 20 seconds. Adopt this habit and reduce that screen-induced strain!

You've been reading textbooks and typing away for hours. Your neck feels stiff, your back is protesting, and your legs are practically begging for some movement. That's when you know it's time for a study break. Take a moment to stretch. Stand up, roll your shoulders, reach for the sky, and twist gently from side to side. Heck, get into child's pose or do a few squats. Your body will thank you. These simple stretches will help release tension and improve your concentration. (Workout Ideas, 2023)

Compound Exercises - Your Go-To Shortlist

Compound exercises are your best friends for an intense at-home workout. They engage multiple muscle groups at once, making your workouts efficient and effective. Plus, you don't need fancy equipment. Here are some moves to try:

Squats: Want strong legs and a firm booty? Squats are the answer. Keep your back straight, chest up, and squat as if you're sitting in an invisible chair.

Planks: Strengthen your core, arms, and shoulders with planks. Hold your body in a straight line, like a plank, on your elbows and toes. Challenge yourself to hold it longer each time.

Core Exercises: A strong core is essential. Think sit-ups, leg raises, or bicycle crunches. These exercises work wonders for your abs.

Yoga: Yoga is a fantastic way to build flexibility, balance, and strength. Plus, it's a calming practice that can help you de-stress after a demanding study session.

Non-Running Cardio: Not a fan of running? No problem! Try jumping jacks, high knees, mountain climbers, or a stairmaster. They get your heart rate up without the need for a treadmill (Workout Ideas, 2023)

Wellness Apps To Check Out

In the fast-paced world we live in, staying healthy can be a challenge. So let's tackle that stress with more tools! These apps are like having a personal trainer and nutritionist rolled into one but without the hefty price tag. They're designed to fit seamlessly into your busy life, so you can stay on top of your fitness goals and overall well-being.

MyFitnessPal: This app is like having a personal nutritionist and fitness coach right in your pocket. It helps you keep tabs on your meals, tracks your calorie intake, and offers exercise routines.

The J&J Official 7-Minute Workout: This app guides you through quick, effective workouts that you can do virtually anywhere. Even with a hectic schedule, you can squeeze in these seven-minute workouts to keep your energy levels up and your stress levels down. (Fitness Apps For Your Best Workout, 2020)

Sworkit: Sworkit is all about customization. Whether you prefer yoga, strength training, or cardio exercises, Sworkit lets you create your workout plans based on your goals and available time. (Kilic, 2018)

Pro tip: Most people find that exercise is best practiced as a HABIT. Fancy equipment, apps and workout gear will out get you so far. I myself find apps for organization and collaborating far for important than apps for exercise! For most people habit stacking their exercise or blocking off times on their calendar —and committing to invest that time in their health and self-care- are the real secrets to success. Seeing a running theme in this book?

Now it's time for the ***Chapter 5 Worksheet***, where you'll identify your values. By understanding your values you can make choices that empower you. This is actually part of a smart strategy for stress management, to keep your mind and body healthy!

Alright, we've covered a lot in this chapter! We explored mental well-being, self-care, nutrition, meals, and physical fitness. Now, let's explore the next chapter on "Nurturing Creativity," and consider different ways to get the most out of our adventures that lie ahead!

Chapter 6
Why Creativity Is Powerful

"The world always seems brighter when you've just made something that wasn't there before."

-Neil Gaiman

Creation is joy!

I'm thrilled to be diving into this next chapter with you, because it's all about embracing the wonderful power of creativity and watching it flourish in your life.

Many people get frustrated by the common challenge of getting into that revered "state of flow", but there are tools and techniques to overcome obstacles to that.

So, are you ready to spark your inner creative, fan the flames of your ideas, and embrace the key to unlocking your most creative abilities?

Embrace Creative Thinking

We tend to associate creativity with certain jobs and fields of study. You know, the kind where people wear funky hats, scribble in notebooks, and talk about their "process" a lot. But the reality is that creativity is useful in all kinds of work. Whether you're studying engineering, business, or even neuroscience, creativity can be your secret weapon, adding a splash of innovation to your endeavors. And here's the best part: you can become more creative, even if you don't think of yourself as a creative person. (Patterson, 2020).

So, before we dive headfirst into this creative pool, let's define what we're talking about. Creativity isn't only for painting masterpieces or composing symphonies; it's also about thinking differently, solving problems in new ways, and seeing opportunities where others might miss them.

Envision yourself as the one who transforms an industry, resolves intricate issues in a novel way, or brings twists, color, or humor to the mundane. That's the power of creativity, and it's a skill that can open doors you didn't even know existed.

Creativity isn't confined to art studios. Regardless of your interests, you can infuse creativity into your school and work activities and goals. Be prepared to think outside the box and bring fresh perspectives to your coursework. Whether you're engineering solutions or interpreting Shakespearean sonnets, creativity is your secret sauce. Join art clubs, collaborate across disciplines, attend creative workshops, and keep a creative journal. Courage, curiosity and a genuine effort will reveal the creative within you, even if you've never picked up a paintbrush. (Park et al., 2021)

Why Creativity Matters

Alright, let's dive even deeper into the mesmerizing world of creativity and why it's not just a nifty side skill but an absolute game-changer in your educational journey and beyond. Buckle up because creativity is about to take center stage, and you'll soon realize it's a brilliant skill for excelling in higher education and making your mark in the professional world. (EdSurge, 2023).

See it this way: You've just started a new training program, and the first months might feel like a breeze. You memorize facts, regurgitate information, and, well, do what you need to pass those entry-level courses. But here's the twist – as you progress in your academic journey, things change. The courses become more challenging and more demanding. They don't just want you to parrot facts; they want you to think creatively. They're nudging you to step outside the box, to go beyond the surface level of knowledge.

Why is this shift happening, you ask? Well, it's simple. Higher-level courses are designed to push your intellectual boundaries. They want to see if you can connect the dots, solve complex problems, and generate fresh ideas. It's all about beefing up that creative thinking muscle of yours. After all, when you're faced with a real-world problem, chances are it won't be a simple regurgitation task. It'll require you to flex your creative muscles and devise innovative solutions. But let's not stop there.

The Professional Benefits of Creativity

Creativity isn't just a flashy skill you can use to dazzle your bosses or professors; it's a game-changer in your future career. Imagine this: You've finished your initial education, and you're stepping into the professional world. If you want to stand out, to be the individual who devises ingenious solutions to unique problems, creativity is your secret weapon. (Williams, 2022)

Picture this scenario: As technology advances, many routine and repetitive tasks are getting automated. So, where does that leave you? Right at the crossroads where creativity becomes your superpower. It's the X-factor that sets you apart from the competition. While others may rely solely on their hard work, you'll complement your diligence with a dose of creative brilliance. Creativity enables you to tackle novel problems, think outside the box, and devise ingenious solutions that others might overlook. In a world where automation is poised to replace mundane tasks, creativity becomes your superpower.

Now, let's clarify something important. Creativity isn't here to replace hard work; it's here to amplify it. Deliberate and habitual practice is still an essential ingredient in mastering your ability to complete tasks with great results. The role creativity has is to turbocharge your efforts, propelling you from good to exceptional.

Tools and Practices for Creative Expression

Now that we've established why creativity is your secret weapon in your education and beyond, let's get down to the nitty-gritty. How can you harness your creativity? I'm about to unveil an arsenal of 10 tools and practices that will turn you into a creative powerhouse. (Lumen Learning, 2012)

"Creative" and "Non-creative" Is a False Dichotomy

First things first, let's dispel a common myth: the idea that some people are naturally creative while others aren't. The truth? Creativity isn't a binary switch; it's a spectrum. And you, my friend, fall somewhere on that spectrum. The good news? You can shift towards the creative end through practice and the right mindset. Dive into the wisdom shared by Thomas Frank in College Info Geek to discover the nuances of creativity. (College Info Geek, n.d.).

Lay Aside Your Assumptions

Creativity thrives in the realm of the unknown. It's like exploring undiscovered places. So, don't let assumptions and preconceived notions clip your creative wings. Let go of your expectations, and embrace the freedom to think beyond the ordinary. Edutopia has some excellent insights into breaking free from the shackles of assumptions. (Edutopia, 2019).

Take Breaks

Creativity isn't a never-ending sprint; it's more like a delightful dance. And every good dancer knows the importance of breaks. When you're working on a creative project, don't forget to pause and recharge. Life can be a whirlwind, and you might find yourself racing against time. But remember, the most creative ideas often come when you allow your mind to breathe. (Lumen Learning, 2019).

Find Your Most Creative Time of Day

Are you a night owl with a creative burst at midnight, or do you shine like a supernova in the morning? Discover your creative prime time and tailor your creative pursuits to those hours. Your brain is like a well-tuned instrument, and it plays its sweetest melodies at specific times (CELT, 2023).

Use Drawing and Mind-Mapping

Don't underestimate the power of visuals in kindling your creativity. Drawing and mind-mapping are like the magic wands of creative expression. They help you visualize ideas, connect the dots, and uncover hidden patterns. (IDEAs in Action, 2023).

There's been many times in my life where I've hit a creative wall. It happens to everyone. Frustration could feel like a constant companion until I discovered the power of mind-mapping. It opened up new pathways in my brain and helped me navigate the creative maze. Finding it was a life-saver and is now one of my go-to tools.

Feed Your Brain New Ideas

Creativity is like a hungry beast—it thrives on new experiences and ideas. So, make it a habit to feed your brain with fresh perspectives. Explore different subjects, read diverse books, and immerse yourself in various cultures. (Lumen Learning, 2019).

Get Bored

Yes, you read that right. Boredom is often the birthplace of creativity. When your mind isn't constantly engaged with stimuli, it starts generating its own. So, don't be afraid to embrace boredom. It's a way to allow your mind to say, "Hey, let's create something interesting!" (CELT, 2023)

Have Stimulating Conversations

Conversations are like intellectual sparks that ignite your creative fire. Engage in stimulating discussions with friends, professors, or even strangers. The exchange of ideas can lead to unexpected creative breakthroughs. (College Success, 2018).

You Can't Force Creativity, but You Can Encourage It

Lastly, remember that creativity is like a shy friend; you can't force it to show up, but you can create an inviting atmosphere. When you're struggling to make time for it, take a few deep breaths. Give time and attention to restructuring your calendar. Find those thirty-minute pockets of time that had been hiding. Block those off with your note of choice. It might be: "Scribble." Cultivate a mindset of openness, curiosity, and wonder. Allow your creativity to flourish naturally.

(Lumen Learning, 2019). Fortunately, the fact will always remain: creation is joy - and that fact does not change with time.

How to Maintain a Creative Practice

Maintaining a creative practice is like nurturing a garden; you need to tend to it regularly to see it flourish. Or if you prefer, think of it as a journey rather than a destination. Don't fixate on the end result; instead, focus on the process. Set aside dedicated time for your creative endeavors, whether it's writing, painting, dancing, or any other form of expression (Pratt Institute, 2022).

You may have come across the saying, "Practice makes perfect" quite a few times in your life. In sixth grade, one of my peers raised his hand and asked our teacher, "If nobody's perfect, why practice?" We all laughed. A young philosopher!

I'm so glad he asked, because the question revealed an answer:

To become better than we were before. Because who doesn't want to be better? Who doesn't want others to get better? And who doesn't want this world to be better? Jerks, that's who. But, I digress.

It turns out that for people and everything to get better, creativity is an essential ingredient. And just as any skill-activity combo requires practice for better results and continued productivity, creativity requires practice for creative outcomes.

Please always remember: There are infinite opportunities for creativity.

Even at this point, some of you might still feel like they're missing the trick. You may wonder, "But really, how should I go about it??"

We've explored the importance of creativity and talked about strategies and tools, but let's explore one more: improving your self-knowledge to keep creativity flowing. Spoiler alert: The more you understand yourself, the more potent your creative expression becomes!

Explore different forms of creativity. You might be afraid to, but remember you're going to practice those powerful skills of courage, curiosity, and creativity! Sign up for a drawing class even if you feel unsure of your ability or the "end result". Try your hand at photography, digital art, pottery, and more. The more you experiment, the more versatile your creative toolkit becomes and the more you'll get to know yourself. There's actually a very high chance you'll discover a hidden talent or passion that's been waiting to burst forth.

My college days were marked by an insatiable urge to write. I didn't produce many literary masterpieces, but there are several I'm still proud of! I wrote assignments more colorfully and flowery than perhaps they needed to be, and established a habit of scribbling thoughts and sketches in journals. Some days it was brilliant; other days, not so much. But the act of showing up for my creative practice was what truly mattered.

Remember, the creative process isn't always smooth sailing. You'll encounter creative blocks, self-doubt, and moments of frustration. But these are all part of the journey. Don't let them discourage you. Instead, see them as challenges to overcome. If you run into one of these obstacles, it's perfectly ok to get inspiration. Do an internet search for "creative prompts". See what happens.

Now, be warned: People with less confidence or enthusiasm can dish all kinds of skeptical garbage, like: "Isn't that lazy?" "But what are you going to do with it?" "But what does it mean?" "But that didn't come from your head." "It's not exactly original."

YUCK. Am I right?

When you hear any garbage like this about your creative efforts, or any other thing you're practicing, do you know what to do? You go seek out and find responses from the equally if-not-more numerous people in this world who value creativity and effort. Their answers will sound something like these:

"Haha, I like it!", "Hey, your inner artist!", "Wow, I love it!", "Oo, it makes me think of _______!", "Sweet! Are you doing stuff like this consistently?", or "I want to see more!"

Keep experimenting, stay curious, and remember that creativity can be your constant companion, if you make the time for it. When you continue despite the obstacles, when you constantly push through these hurdles, you emerge as a more resilient and creative individual.

I don't care if it's on the bus, after dinnertime, after showering, or under the cover of darkness! (Interesting habit stacking idea?) Don't! Give! Up!

Believe this and put it to the test: Trying out new creative techniques, learning about yourself, and nurturing your creative practice by using your skills habitually will help to bring you joy and success in life.

In the next powerful chapter, "Nurturing Social Relationships," I'll help you figure out how to bring your authentic self into your interactions with others to help create meaningful connections. These will form some of those building blocks you can use to create your dream life!

PART II

The Social Spark

Chapter 7
Nurturing
Social
Relationships

"Life is beautiful not because of the things we see or do,
but because of the people we meet."

-Simon Sinek

As we transition through new phases of life, remember that school and work are about much more than academics and completing tasks.

They're spaces for forging friendships, nurturing connections with cherished ones, and networking for the future.

The people we connect with in life - our family, friends, and those we meet throughout life's adventures - can make our lives more vibrant, meaningful, and truly wonderful.

So, let's set out on a journey of discovery and learn how to cultivate, cherish, and flourish in these essential relationships that make life worth living.

Finding Your People (It Takes Time)

Ah, the age-old quest for new friends. Whether you're an extrovert, an introvert, or somewhere in between, forging new friendships can be both exciting and challenging. Here are some tips for making friends at school and at work, based on my experiences and the experiences of others. They ought to help you bond over late-night pizza runs, inside jokes, and interesting future adventures in no time. (Paonita, 2023)

Just remember, Rome wasn't built in a day, and neither are friendships. Finding your tribe might not happen overnight, and that's perfectly okay. Building lasting connections is a journey, not a destination. So, don't be discouraged if your social circle doesn't resemble a blockbuster movie montage right away. Practice using your powerful life skills with these strategies for meeting more people, and watch as your life-long friend-making game grows strong! (Gordon, 2023)

Tips to Making New Friends in School and At Work

Engage with Classmates and Coworkers

Potential friends may surround you in your classes or workplace. Strike up conversations about assignments, share notes, or team up for group projects. That awkward group project partner might just turn into your lifelong buddy. (Warmington, 2021)

Get a Study Partner

Studying can be a solitary affair, but it doesn't have to be. Find a study partner who shares your academic interests. You'll not only ace those exams together but also form a formidable friendship bond.

Attend Events

Schools (and cities) are like social hubs with events happening left, right, and center. Attend lectures, seminars, club meetings, and any other shindigs that pique your curiosity. You never know when you'll stumble upon your future best friend at a live music event, a poetry slam night or a science expo.

Work on Campus

Looking for a part-time job? Why not work on campus? Whether you're in the library, cafeteria, or the campus radio station, working alongside peers is an excellent way to make friends.

Connect with Other Students Online

In the digital age, connecting online can be as viable and enjoyable as in-person interactions. Join topic-specific social media groups or forums where students discuss everything from campus events to crafting. It's a fantastic way to break the ice before meeting face-to-face.

What If You Are Introverted or Shy?

For those who are shy or introverted, making friends might seem like a Herculean task. But fear not, introverts – school is the perfect playground for forming meaningful connections. Here are some tailored tips:

Set Goals: Challenge yourself with achievable social goals. Start small, like initiating a conversation with one new person each day.

Introduce Yourself: When you're in a new environment, a simple "Hi, I'm [Your Name]" can go a long way in breaking the ice.

Make Eye Contact: Eye contact shows you're engaged and interested in the conversation. It's a subtle yet effective way to build rapport.

Host People: Invite classmates or dorm neighbors to low-key gatherings like movie nights or study sessions. This takes off the pressure of large social events.

Don't Make Excuses: It's easy to make excuses to avoid social situations, but challenge yourself to step out of your comfort zone.

Avoid Worrying: Remember, everyone is navigating this social maze in their own way! Don't worry too much about what others think, and focus on being your authentic self. (Leach, 2018)

So, there you have it, fellow explorers – a wealth of ideas to start your friend-seeking journey. Making friends is exciting and with a little courage and curiosity, you'll create wonderful memories.

Building Confidence in Friendships

Making friends, keeping them, and ensuring your relationships are as robust as your life's dreams can be a challenge. But fear not, my friend, because I'm here to help you become a friendship aficionado.

The first essential skill? Be friendly toward everyone. Remember that friendship opportunities are everywhere, even in unexpected places. Be friendly and open to interactions with everyone you encounter, from your roommate to the person standing next to you in the cafeteria line.

Forming, Storming, Norming, and Performing

I was in my first semester, meeting new people left and right, and everything felt like sunshine and rainbows - that's what I like to call the "Forming" stage. But then, brace yourselves for the "Storming" stage. It's like the plot twists in a dramatic play- conflicts and differences cropped up out of nowhere. I'm talking disagreements over pizza toppings, late-night noise, and who gets control of the TV remote.

But hang in there because the story doesn't end there. After the "Storming" comes the "Norming" stage. It's when you all start to understand each other better, find common ground, and create your own unique group culture. You learn to compromise on the pizza, take turns with the remote, and even find a rhythm for those late-night antics.

And finally, we've got the "Performing" stage. It's like when your favorite band is in perfect harmony on stage, nailing every note and move. In your friendship ensemble, this is when you're all in sync, supporting each other, and having a blast together. (Six Sigma Daily, 2020)

Bonding (through Respect, Empathy & Curiosity)

Now, let's talk about the secret sauce of friendships: bonding. It's like making a sandwich – you need all the right ingredients to create something delightful. Respect, empathy, and curiosity are your BFF ingredients. Respect is the foundation; it's treating your friends like the royalty they are. Empathy is the ability to step into their shoes, even if they're going through things you don't fully understand. And curiosity in friendships? Well, that's the spice that keeps your friendships exciting. Ask questions, be genuinely interested in their stories, and you'll see how your bonds deepen faster than a plot twist in a thriller novel.

Be Confident in What You Bring to Friendships

Now, let's get personal. Confidence is your best friend's best friend. Think about it – you bring something unique to every friendship table, just like a potluck dinner where everyone's got their signature dish. Be confident that your qualities make you a good friend. This includes your killer sense of humor, your epic taste in music, or your ability to solve mysteries like Sherlock Holmes. Embrace your quirks, and soon enough, others will appreciate the flavor you add to their lives.

Setting Healthy Boundaries (Say "No" When You Need to)

Lastly, let's talk about boundaries again. They're like the guardrails on the friendship highway, keeping things safe and steady. It's crucial to set healthy boundaries and say "no" when needed. Remember, you're not a 24/7 superhero; you're a human with your own needs, limitations, and tv series to binge-watch. Saying "no" isn't a rejection; it's a way of respecting your own limits and maintaining your well-being. It's self-care, remember?

Staying in Touch with Friends Who Are Far Away

Just because you're miles apart doesn't mean you have to lose touch with your buddies from back home. In fact, with the power of technology and a sprinkle of effort, you can make sure your friendships remain as strong as ever.

First off, let's embrace the wonders of the digital age. I'm talking about video calls, folks! Platforms like Zoom, Skype, or good ol' FaceTime can turn your regular chats into full-blown virtual hangouts. Schedule some catch-up sessions with your pals, grab your favorite snacks, and have a blast sharing stories about your school and social escapades. (Ramsdell, 2021)

But hey, don't underestimate the power of a heartfelt or meme-laden text chat either. Sometimes, it's those little moments of connection that matter most. So, keep those messages flowing. Share memes, updates, and inside jokes. It's like having an ongoing conversation that never really ends.

Oh, and here's a pro tip: Surprise them with a handwritten letter or a care package once in a while. Trust me, there's something magical about receiving tangible, snail-mail love. It shows you've put extra thought and effort into maintaining the friendship, and it's a fantastic way to keep the bond strong.

Lastly, plan reunions or trips if you can swing it. It doesn't have to be extravagant; even a weekend getaway can do wonders for rekindling those friendships. Plus, it gives you something to look forward to! (Undergraduate Programs, 2021)

Just remember, it's all about making the effort, staying in touch in your own unique way, and cherishing the moments you share, no matter the distance.

Staying in Touch with Your Roots

At times, coping with school or work life can be trickier than you imagined. You may start to miss your friends, your family, and that cozy feeling of familiarity. Suddenly, you may be faced with the FOMO monster, thinking you're missing out on all the fun back home. That's why, my fellow collegiate explorers, staying connected is a skill to learn, no matter where your academic journey takes you (The Jed Foundation, 2023)

Now, let's dive into 6 socially savvy ideas to keep those bonds with your nearest and dearest intact:

1. Schedule Chats In Advance: Some find it helpful to plan phone calls with loved ones ahead of time, in order to reduce anxiety. For many, it's like a digital dose of comfort food for the soul.

2. Throw a Video Party: Spice things up by hosting a virtual video hangout. It's like having a family dinner without leaving your dorm room.

3. Watch Your Favorite Shows Together: Distance can't stop you from enjoying a binge-watching session with your friends or loved ones. Pick a show, hit play at the same time, and voilà, you're virtually together!

4. Send Them Things That Remind You of Them: Surprise your loved ones with thoughtful care packages or postcards. It's a tangible way to let them know you're thinking of them.

5. Meet in the Middle: If you live relatively close to home and you want to maintain face-to-face connections, you may find it helpful to plan weekend meetups mid-way between your locations.

6. Surprise Visits: Nothing beats the element of surprise. If the opportunity arises, pay your family an unexpected visit, and let their reaction speak for itself. (Undergraduate Programs, 2021)

Alright, let's wrap up this chapter with a quick recap and some key takeaways. In "Tips to Making New Friends," we delved into the art of making connections, finding your people, and building confidence in friendships. Remember the stages of Forming, Storming, Norming, and Performing? They're your pathway to thriving social circles.

Now, get ready for the next chapter – it's all about balancing responsibilities while having a blast. We'll explore different forms of fun, how to make the most of your budget, and share tips for establishing that golden work-life balance. So, if you're itching for some recreational activities to build into your dream life, stick around!

Chapter 8
Finding Fun

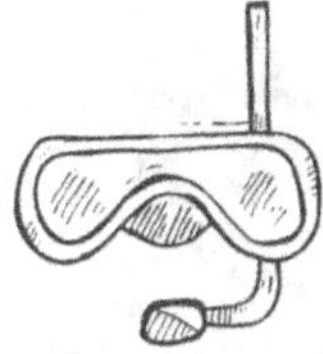

Welcome to a quick chapter that's all about the good stuff – finding fun and making the most of your educational experience. As Tony Robbins aptly puts it, life is for living, and your school and work years are no exception. Amidst the times of work, struggle and uncertainty, there's still countless opportunities for excitement, joy, and unforgettable moments waiting for you. But striking the balance requires powerful skills!

One of the most enjoyable aspects of fun experiences is that their appearance in your life will often look completely different than you expect, and in the most unexpected places. What could make fun even better? When it doesn't empty your wallet!

Spending Smart for Maximum Fun

I get it! You're probably on a budget, juggling coursework, daily expenses, tuition, or perhaps a job. Perhaps all of these and more. But that doesn't mean you can't have a blast without breaking the bank. In fact, there are some clever ways to have fun on the cheap. Here are some of my favorite ideas and trust me, they're not just budget-friendly. They'll give you the awesome tingly feelings of fun!

Change and Idea Jars

Picture this—a jar filled with spare change, and another one brimming with exciting, low-cost ideas. When the change jar's full, pick a creative idea from the other jar and see what you can do with the coins you've saved. It's an easy way to bond with your roomie, have fun and be thrifty all at once.

I remember when my roomie and I used to have a "change jar challenge." We'd fill it up with spare change, pick a fun idea, and see how much we could do with the coins. Let me tell you, some of our craziest and most memorable experiences came from mere dollars!

Student Discounts

Your student ID is your golden ticket to savings. Don't forget to cash in on student discounts when subscribing to streaming services and apps you may want to try. Also, keep an eye out for student discounts at local eateries.

Book-to-Movie Nights

Who says reading and entertainment can't go hand in hand? Read a book with your friends and then stream the movie adaptation. It's a fantastic way to dive into great stories with friends in a more meaningful way.

Campus and Work Performances & Events

Your school or work life is often brimming with creative talent. Check out one-act plays, choral shows, or band concerts put on by your fellow students. Some of these events are free, and others offer discounted tickets to students. Coworkers may perform at events, run cool fundraising events, or give talks promoting their new side hustles. Support them and have fun new experiences all at once!

Garage Sale Adventures

If your town hosts garage sales, seize the opportunity. Garage sales can be an amusing way to spend a weekend exploring your town with friends. There's fun to be had spending time together, whether immersed in "junk" or treasures!

Thrifting

For the budget-savvy shopaholic, thrift stores are a treasure trove. Scour local thrift shops or the clearance sections at larger stores with friends for fabulous fashion finds.

Farmers' Market Fun: If your town has a farmers' market, make it a point to visit. You'll discover crafts, baked goods, live music, and more. And if you're a savvy negotiator, you might even haggle your way to great deals.

Dollar Store Dates: Here's a fun and budget-friendly idea. Each person gets a theme (search the web if you're stumped), set a dollar limit, and meet up after 15-20 minutes to share your finds. If you love it, buy it. If not, it goes back on the shelf. It's really about having fun on a dime.

Outdoor Adventures

Plan a picnic or embark on an outdoor adventure with your friends. Whether it's hiking, biking, or simply basking in the sun, Mother Nature has so much to offer.

Staycation

Can't travel far? No problem! Plan a staycation right in your town or dorm with your roommates or pals. Explore local attractions, try new restaurants, or have a spa or movie night, and create lasting memories.

Trivia Nights

Put your knowledge to the test at local trivia nights hosted by student organizations or businesses. It's a fantastic way to geek out and have fun.

Arcades

Embrace your inner child at arcades. A pocketful of quarters can go a long way, providing hours of amusement.

Food Festivals

If you're a foodie, seek out local food festivals. These culinary events are not only delicious but also a whole lot of fun. (College Dorm Life, n.d.)

These are just a few ideas to kickstart your budget-friendly fun adventures. Remember that fun is an important part of your early adulting experience, and you'll get to choose how to make the most of it!

In this chapter, we've explored different forms of fun, from joining clubs and attending events to embracing the great outdoors. You know that school isn't just about studying and work; it's about expanding your horizons and creating memories that'll last a lifetime. This includes things like going on a hike with friends, dancing at a concert, or playing board games. It's all great stuff.

Now, let's transition into the next chapter, where we'll dive into dorm life. I'm going to help equip you with the essential must-knows before you start a dorm life journey. From creating your dorm checklist and staying organized in a shared space to top qualities to adopt when living with others – it's all part of growing into your dream life!

You've got this!

Chapter 9
Planning For Dorm Life

If you plan to step into the dynamic and communal space of a dorm room, you'll be stumbling upon new experiences, challenges, and unforgettable memories.

In this chapter, we'll delve into the art of navigating dorm life, exploring everything from making your dorm room a cozy haven to fostering great roommate relationships.

Powerful Must-knows Before You Start Your Dorm Life

The excitement of newfound independence mixed with the challenges of shared living spaces can be quite the rollercoaster ride. But don't stress, my dorm dwellers, because I've got some invaluable must-knows to help you navigate dorm life with grace.

Establish Guidelines with Your Roommate(s)

In those first few weeks, sit down with your roommate(s) and set some ground rules. Trust me; it'll save you from potential roommate drama down the road. Remember, compromise is your best friend. I once had a roommate who thought playing music loudly while she studied just outside our room was a great idea. Needless to say, we quickly established some noise-level boundaries.

Invest in a Good Set of Headphones

When you're sharing a living space, noise can become the enemy of peace. Invest in quality headphones to escape into your own world when needed and to avoid becoming the noisy neighbor yourself.

Make Your Bed in the Morning

It might sound trivial, but making your bed can set a calm tone for your crazy day ahead. Plus, coming back to a bed that's made and a tidy room after a long day of classes is surprisingly comforting.

Don't Sacrifice Practicality for a Cool Room

Sure, Pinterest-worthy dorm rooms are tempting, but remember that functionality trumps aesthetics. Space is precious, so choose furniture and decor that serves a purpose.

Be Prepared with Necessities

Trust me, getting sick at school is no more fun than back home. Stock up on basic necessities like tissues, pain relievers, and a thermometer. When the flu strikes, you'll thank yourself. (Great Value Colleges, 2023)

Closet Space is Limited

College closets are notorious for being compact. Bring only what you truly need, and consider space-saving storage solutions like under-bed bins.

Participate in Dorm Events

Don't be a hermit! Dorm events are a fantastic way to meet people, make friends, and build a sense of community. Plus, who can resist free pizza night?

Find Time to Organize Early On

The chaos of moving in can be overwhelming, but don't procrastinate on organizing your space. Tackle it early, and you'll thank yourself later when everything has its place.

Don't Trust Everyone

While school is a time to make lifelong friends, exercise caution. Not everyone you meet will have your best interests at heart. Keep your valuables secure, and trust your instincts.

Buy Multi-Purpose Products

Space in a dorm room is a hot commodity. Opt for multi-purpose products like a bed with built-in storage or a combination microwave-convection oven to save precious square footage. (College Dorm Life, 2023)

And there you have it – your quick-start guide for thriving in a dorm life. Remember, school is about learning both inside and outside the classroom, and your dorm is where some of your most cherished memories will be made. Embrace the experience, and enjoy the journey!

Top Qualities to Adopt for Living with Others

Let's talk about the powerful skills you'll need to nail learning this whole adulting gig. Because don't forget, everything involving others that you do, try, and learn has the power to inspire and create your dream life down the road!

Communication – and no, I'm not talking about just adding emojis to your texts! I mean open, honest, and empathetic chats that'll help you avoid those awkward roommate tiffs and turn conflicts into constructive solutions.

Respect – it's like the golden rule of life. Respect personal boundaries, beliefs, and quirks, so that everyone feels valued and cozy in their own skin. This is how you create that magical vibe of togetherness.

Patience – is your secret weapon for surviving those late-night study sessions and shared living spaces. When your roomie's quirks start to get under your skin, channel your inner Zen master and remember that patience keeps the peace.

Adaptability – aka the ability to roll with the punches, is one of your new skills to practice with gusto. Whether it's adjusting to surprise dorm inspections or your roommate's unexpected party, flexibility is key for fostering your ability to stay calm.

Kindness and consideration – They're not just for your grandma to nag you about. Spread 'em around, and watch the positive vibes ripple through your living situation. And last but not least, cleanliness and organization – yep, they do matter. Keep your space tidy, and you'll create a haven that benefits everyone under your roof. (Rebecca, 2023)

Staying Organized: Mastering the Art of Dorm Life

Keeping your living space organized can improve your college experience. Whether you're new to campus or a seasoned dorm dweller, try these tips to keep your space in order.

Let's dive right into it. Picture your dorm room – cozy, compact, and your own little slice of college heaven. Now, imagine this: You're standing at the threshold with all your bags, ready to take on this new adventure. What's the answer to keeping this snug space both functional and fabulous? It all begins with some savvy organization.

Make a List, Check It Twice

You know, it's funny how something as simple as making a list can make a world of difference. I'm talking about essentials like a shower caddy, containers, and closet organizers. You might need them for communal bathrooms or to maximize your space, or to safeguard your valuables or to unleash your creative side.

Trust me, these things can be your lifeline during those hectic first weeks of college. Why not give it a shot and create a checklist to guide you? (Sandoval, 2021) Just make sure you don't get carried away. This isn't a shopping spree, and you don't need every fancy gadget on the market. Tailor your list to your personal needs and preferences. If you're an artist, those art supplies will be part of your self-care habits. If you're a neat freak, those containers will be your container-y best friends. Think of it as assembling your arsenal of dorm life essentials, each item with a specific mission to keep you sane and focused.

Why Stay Organized?

Before you reject the notion of arranging your dorm room, think about this: Having an orderly living area can improve your efficiency, decrease anxiety, and make a refuge where you can take a break and recharge. Plus, it's an excellent way to make a good impression on your roommate(s) and keep the peace in tight quarters. (Sandoval, 2021)

Before we wrap up our talk on staying organized, let's zoom out for a moment and take in the whole view.

So far, we've covered must-knows before you embark on your dorm life adventure and the top qualities to adopt for harmonious living with others. We've discussed the importance of clear communication, empathy, and respect in roommate relationships.

Now, as we venture into the next chapter, brace yourself for a guide on apartment selection, landlord research, and housemate selection. I'll offer some tools for how to conduct a successful apartment search, find compatible housemate(s) and maintain a respectful relationship with them.

Prepare to expect the unexpected and remember that each challenge is an opportunity to grow into the person you want to be! The powerful skills you put to practice day after day, month after month, have the power to help you do just that. What do you say to becoming brighter, more calm, more patient, stronger, and happier? Sounds to me like you're well on your way to creating your dream life!

Chapter 10
Powerful Skills for Shared Living

"It isn't where you came from. It's where you're going that counts."

-Ella Fitzgerald

Starting your journey in apartment living can feel like embarking on an epic adventure. It's a milestone that signifies freedom, a whole lot of personal responsibility, and unknowable lessons on independence. In this chapter, you'll learn about apartment living and how to make it your own.

I've got tips and insights to ensure your experience is positive and authentic. From understanding your lease agreement to transforming your apartment into a cozy haven, we've got you covered.

So, let's embark on this exciting journey of apartment living with Ella Fitzgerald's wisdom as our guiding star.

Apartment Search, Landlord Research, and Roommate Selection

Alright, it's time to dive into the thrilling world of apartment hunting, landlord detective work, and housemate matchmaking. Think of this as real-life episodes of house-hunting meets your favorite reality show, but with less drama and more practical tips.

How to Conduct an Apartment Search

So, you've decided it's time to break free from dorm life or your childhood home and venture into the world of apartment living. Trust me, I've been there. Let me share a valuable piece of advice from then, it all begins with a well-thought-out strategy. So, step one, get a handle on your budget. What can you comfortably afford without dipping into your weekly pad thai and toilet paper funds?

Once you've got a budget in mind, it's time to hit the internet. Websites like Craigslist, Zillow, or good ol' Google Maps can be your trusty sidekicks in this adventure. Filter your searches based on location, price, and amenities. Pay attention to photos! They can give you a sneak peek into your potential new digs. (Bortz, 2018)

Now, here's where the detective hat comes on. Research your potential landlord. Look up their name or the property management company. You'd be surprised what you can dig up – reviews, horror stories, or even glowing recommendations. It's like your own little episode of CSI: Landlord Edition. But, seriously, this step can save you from potential renting disasters.

How to Find and Choose Potential Housemates

Now, let's talk about housemate(s). Living solo can be expensive, and let's face it, sharing rent and bills is just plain practical. But how do you find the perfect housemate(s)? Well, it's a bit like online dating – you need to chat for a while to determine true compatibility.

Start with your social circle. People you know, like, or think are nice could be potential roomies. Don't underestimate the power of living with someone you already know and like.

If your social network doesn't yield any prospects, turn to the virtual world. Websites like Roommates.com, Craigslist, or even Facebook groups for your university can connect you with potential roommates. Just remember to meet them in person before sealing the deal. If the landlord allows it, maybe opt for a 6-month rather than a 1-year lease, so you can try it out and make sure it's right for you. (How to find a college roommate, n.d.)

There's been a couple of times in my life when I was feeling extra brave, and decided to take a chance on three complete strangers as housemates - talk about navigating new experiences! Beforehand I queried about everything, from their daily routine to their quirks and deal-breakers. Did they burn the midnight oil while I was an early riser? What did they do for fun? How did they plan on using common spaces? These were the kinds of crucial details I needed to uncover.

The Powerful "A to Z" Highlights When It Comes To Shared Living

When it comes to living with others, here's a powerful A to Z creation to help you navigate the waves of shared living experiences. Let it be your insightful guide to harmonious cohabitation!

A is for Agreement: Establish ground rules and expectations before unpacking your bags to prevent future conflicts.

B is for Bills: Utility bills, rent, and groceries are part of the deal. Plan responsibilities and use apps like Splitwise for easy tracking.

C is for Communication: Open dialogue is vital. Don't expect mind-reading abilities; address concerns through friendly chats.

D is for Dishes: Avoid the Leaning Tower of Dishes by setting up a schedule or investing in a dishwasher.

E is for Expectations: Keep expectations realistic; no one's perfect, including yourself.

F is for Food: Sharing is caring, but respect each other's food boundaries.

G is for Guests: Establish guest rules to avoid unexpected sleepovers turning your living room into a hotel.

H is for Harmony: Find a balance between personal space and communal areas.

I is for Issues: Don't let conflicts simmer; address them calmly and rationally.

J is for Journey: Treat this living arrangement as a journey of experiences and lessons.

K is for Keys: Don't forget your keys to avoid 2 a.m. lockouts.

L is for Laughter: Embrace the joy of living together, sharing laughter and creating lasting memories.

M is for Maintenance: Keep your space clean and tidy; chores may not be fun, but they're necessary.

N is for Noise: Respect quiet hours, especially during exams or sleep time.

O is for Open-mindedness: Be open to new experiences and perspectives.

P is for Privacy: Respect your roomie's privacy and expect the same in return.

Q is for Quick Fixes: Learn basic DIY skills for household quick fixes.

R is for Respect: The golden rule of apartment living; treat others as you want to be treated.

S is for Space: Personal space is sacred; always ask permission before invading it.

T is for Time Management: Be mindful of roommates' schedules; avoid epic showers during their rush hours.

U is for Understanding: Try to understand your roommates' quirks and idiosyncrasies.

V is for Ventilation: When cooking aromatic dishes, crack a window or two for ventilation.

W is for Welcome: Create a welcoming and inviting space for yourself and your guests.

X is for X-factor: Every living situation has its unique factor; embrace it as part of the journey.

Y is for Yes... Sometimes: Say yes to new experiences and bonding activities.

Z is for Zen: Make your home a peaceful sanctuary amidst the chaos of the world. Enjoy the ride! (Renting with other people, n.d.)

Life with housemates can be a thrilling journey packed with knowledge, development, and likely a few movie marathons. Embrace it, enjoy it, stay strong and laugh at the unexpected moments along the way.

More On Maintaining A Respectful Relationship With Your Housemate

Having housemates can be a lot of fun, but there can also be difficulties. It's like you are creating a small society inside your apartment. To make sure that everyone feels content and comfortable living there, here's more insight into what you need to know to have a respectful relationship with your housemates.

1. **Great Expectations**: No, not the novel. Start by setting expectations. It's like the ground rules for your shared space. Discuss chores, quiet hours, visitors, and anything else that might be important to you. This way, you're all on the same page from the get-go.

2. **The Art of Listening**: Communication is key. If something's bugging you or if you're feeling uneasy about something your housemate did, talk it out. Be a good listener too; your housemates might have their own concerns or ideas.

3. **Roomie Respect**: It's your home, but it's theirs too. Respect their personal space and belongings. It's like a 'no entry' sign, but without the actual sign.

4. **Crisis Management**: Sometimes, things might go south. Don't let small issues snowball into big ones. Address problems as they come up. It's like dealing with weeds in your garden before they take over.

5. **Social Shenanigans**: Hosting a party? Great! Just check in with your housemates first. Giving them a heads-up is key, so they can choose whether to join the fun or plan their own quiet evening.

6. **The Sticky Note Solution**: Sometimes, it's the little things – like labeling your food or leaving friendly sticky notes wishing them a nice day – that can go a long way in maintaining harmony. (UWYO, 2023)

So, here we are, having explored the ins and outs of finding your apartment haven and living harmoniously with others. You've learned how to conduct a savvy apartment search, research your potential landlord, and pick housemates who'll make your journey even more enjoyable. We've covered the A to Z of apartment living, emphasizing the importance of respect and open communication.

Our next stop: Dating & Your Dream Life...

As we move through this chapter, remember that creating your dream life also requires honing your powerful skills in close relationships. We'll consider what readiness for dating might look like, how to make sure you're in a healthy relationship, and how self-awareness and communication are your keys to success!

Ready for this next exciting chapter?

Chapter 11
Dating and Your Dream Life

"When someone tells me "no," it doesn't mean I can't do it, it simply means I can't do it with them."

-Karen E. Quinones Miller

Life is going to be full of many unfamiliar experiences, from new forms of education to hanging out with new friends, and from making important decisions autonomously to having all the responsibilities of a grownup. But perhaps one of the most exciting and, let's face it, occasionally perplexing aspects of life is starting relationships and dating. It's like stepping into a whole new world of romantic possibilities.

In this chapter, we'll consider balancing the plight for connection and love with your own personal well-being and growth. Healthy and successful relationships are like well-crafted masterpieces; they require passion, love, the powerful three, plus respect, time and effort, to create something beautiful.

You want your life to be filled with strong connections and happiness, but it's equally important to steer clear of relationships that could potentially derail your personal well-being and agency to create your dream life.

Like many others, I've experienced the effort required to focus on relationships – friendships, crushes, romantic involvements, and all the rest. My measure of a great relationship with someone was experiencing mutual attraction, the magic of fun, and the bond of genuine caring, while having the freedom to maintain my personal commitments and work toward my goals. When exploring romantic possibilities, I had to identify when a positive bond could become something less desirable. The truth is, this is something we all need to do when we're out there dating. On the flip side, recognizing and appreciating something good when you have it, is a skill in itself; the skill of gratitude. When you feel and know in your heart that you're creating that masterpiece - baby that's love!

Creating Your Dream Love Life

Now let's consider some insights and advice for the complex, exciting world of dating:

The Ingredients and Skills for Love

Starting a new relationship can be as thrilling as that rollercoaster ride at the amusement park. Love, while incredibly powerful, is just one piece of the relationship puzzle. There's so much more to consider – compatibility, communication, and shared goals, to name a few.

Put Yourself First

First things first, always put yourself at the top of your priority list. It's easy to get swept up in the whirlwind of a new relationship, but remember that your happiness and well-being should never take a back seat. This is something I learned the hard way during my young-adulting days when I sometimes put others' needs ahead of my own. It's essential to take care of yourself first, emotionally and mentally, before embarking on any romantic adventures. (Smith & Medrano, 2019)

You Don't Have to Date

Last but not least, let's debunk the myth that you *have* to date in school or any other phase of life. Some folks choose to focus solely on their studies and personal growth, and that's perfectly fine. There's no one-size-fits-all approach to dating. Do what feels right for you, and remember, it's your dream life to craft. Your dream love life might be one of freedom and close friendships. (Smith & Medrano, 2019)

Ask for What You Need

Communication is key, my friends. Relationships can be a bit like navigating a maze, but clear and open communication can help you find your way. Find your courage to ask for what you need. This could be more space, more time, or more emotional support. Likewise, if something's bothering you, speak up. During my first forays into dating, I often hesitated to address issues with my friends or partners. But guess what? Yep - Keeping things bottled up never solved anything.

If you're not comfortable talking to the person directly, confide in someone you trust. They can offer valuable insights and support. Remember, communication is a two-way street, and it's the key to resolving conflicts and building healthier, happier relationships. (Amherst College, 2006) It's as simple as that.

Your Education Comes First

Repeat after me: Education comes first. While school can be a hub of romantic possibilities, never forget that you're there primarily to learn and grow academically. Balancing your studies and your social life can be a bit of a tightrope act, but remember why you're in school in the first place.

Don't Let Your Relationship Take Over Your Life

Yes, love is beautiful, but it shouldn't consume your every waking moment. Your relationship should complement your life, not replace it. One of my college buddies got so wrapped up in his relationship that he later regretted missing out on some incredible opportunities. Keep your individuality and your passions alive.

It Can Be Isolating

School can sometimes feel like a sea of faces, and the initial excitement might wear off, leaving you feeling a tad lonely. For some people, they try to revive this excitement by retreating into their relationship. This can be completely normal, but it's also a reminder to stay connected with friends, join clubs, and explore your interests beyond your relationship.

It's OK to Break Up With Your High School Significant Other

Our departure for new educational or work opportunities is often the time when high school sweethearts find themselves on diverging paths. It can be tough, but it's entirely okay to break up with your high school significant other if your feelings have changed or if you're growing in different directions. Remember, this is your time to discover who you are and what you want.

Honesty in Your Intentions

Some folks are all about the casual hookups, while others are looking for something a bit more serious. It's crucial to communicate your intentions clearly and to understand your partner's as well. Life is a mixed bag, and everyone's on their unique journey, so just be honest about what you're looking for.

Abuse Might Not Look Like You Think It Will

Whether you're in an educational program or beyond, understanding what makes a relationship thrive is a vital life skill. So let's touch on a heavy one: abuse. It doesn't always come in the form of physical violence. Emotional and psychological abuse can be just as damaging, so recognizing signs of an unhealthy relationship is a real life-saver. If something doesn't feel right, trust your instincts. Seek help and support. No one deserves to be in an abusive relationship.

Maintaining A Healthy Relationship

Now let's be aware of some of the tougher experiences that we can encounter in relationships. Whether you're dealing with a break-up, a long-distance relationship, or a harmful relationship, I've got your back!

When to Say Goodbye

Ending a relationship can be tough, but staying in a bad or unfulfilling one can be even tougher. It's like holding onto a sinking ship when you could be swimming toward a brighter future.

Healing and Moving Forward

Break-ups can feel like a storm cloud over your otherwise sunny life. To cope with heartbreak, seek support from friends, family or mentors, and remember that the most powerful healer of grief is time. Be patient with yourself as time passes and you refocus your life, and you can emerge stronger than ever. I've certainly had my share of heartache, but with time, those dark days turn into valuable life lessons. I'm much clearer on what I have to offer in relationships, and what I'm looking for. You may experience this too. The result? A more powerful, fulfilled and happier you.

Long-Distance Relationships

Long-distance relationships can show how much love people have for each other, but they can also be a test of that strength. Many people find themselves navigating the ups and downs of maintaining a relationship when miles separate them. It's like trying to balance a tightrope walk while juggling textbooks.

Identifying the Red Flags

Sometimes relationships can take a dark turn, with emotional or physical abuse entering the picture. It's a topic we need to address openly and honestly. I remember when a close friend of mine had a tough relationship. At first, she brushed off the subtle signs of control and manipulation, thinking they were just minor quirks. But as time passed, those red flags became more pronounced, and her emotional well-being deteriorated. It was heartbreaking to witness someone I cared about going through such a difficult situation.

Signs to Watch Out For

So, what are these red flags that can help you steer clear of unhealthy relationships?

If you're in an unhealthy relationship, it's important to recognize the signs and take steps to protect yourself. These warning signs can include physical violence, controlling behavior, and explosive outbursts (Relationships 101, n.d.). Let's break them down in plain language:

Privacy Invasion: If someone is constantly checking your cell phone or email without your permission, it's a clear sign of boundary-crossing. I remember having a friend who just couldn't resist asking about my texts. It made me uncomfortable, and rightfully so.

Constant Criticism: Healthy relationships should uplift you, not bring you down. If you're constantly being put down or made to feel inferior, it's time to reevaluate.

Jealousy Overdrive: Sure, a little jealousy can be cute, but extreme jealousy or insecurity is toxic. In college, I knew a couple where one partner couldn't stand the other talking to anyone of the opposite sex. It didn't end well.

Temper Tantrums: Explosive tempers can be a deal-breaker. If someone goes from 0 to 100 over the smallest things, that's a warning sign.

Isolation Tactics: If you find yourself being isolated from friends and family, it's time to ask why. Healthy relationships should never demand that you cut ties with your support network. (Heineman, 2021)

False Accusations: Being falsely accused of things you haven't done can be emotionally draining. If it's happening frequently, take it seriously.

Wild Mood Swings: Relationships should have stability. If your partner's mood swings are causing turbulence, it's worth addressing.

Physical Harm: This one is non-negotiable. No one should ever physically hurt you in any way. Period.

Possessiveness: Healthy relationships involve trust and respect for personal space. Possessiveness is a sign of insecurity.

Control Issues: No one should dictate your every move or tell you what to do. It's your life, after all. (Tips for Healthy Relationships, n.d)

Pressure for Intimacy: Lastly, no one should ever pressure or force you into any sexual activity you're uncomfortable with. Consent is key. (The Art of Maintaining a Healthy Relationship in College, n.d.)

As we wrap up our consideration of successful dating, it's important to remember that relationships should be positive and enriching. We've talked about some of the ingredients for love, emphasized that self-awareness and open communication are your compass, and learned ways to spot and avoid unhealthy relationships.

In the next chapter, let's explore the world of saving, budgeting, and considering Financial Independence, ensuring you're well-prepared for your financial journey.

PART III

**Powerful Skills
to Manage Your Money,
Education & Work Goals**

Chapter 12
Managing Your Money

"Being rich is having money; being wealthy is having time."

-*Margaret Bonanno*

You're becoming powerfully independent! Congratulations on taking this big step towards your future! But with great freedom comes great responsibility, especially when it comes to your finances. Sure, it sounds exciting — and it is! You get to decide where and how to spend your money. No more nagging about curfew or what to eat for dinner. You are the master of your choices. But here's the catch: You also get to experience the consequences of those choices, both the good and the not-so-good.

Fret not! This chapter is to arm you with some incredible financial wisdom that will keep you in excellent financial shape throughout your adulting journey. Hold on to your wallet; it's going to be a wild ride of money matters (minus the stomach-churning plunges)!

Here's one of the biggest "secrets" for success: Financial wisdom isn't only about earning money; it's also about managing what you have efficiently.

Now let's become more powerful with proactive ways to build your financial savvy!

Manage Your Money Like A Pro

Take Control, and Be Responsible

Financial responsibility is the name of the game. It's time to embrace adulthood and make responsible financial choices. Start by watching videos, reading books and articles about saving and investing money. Then every other money-related topic you can handle. Next, set some clear financial goals.

Create a Budget

To achieve your financial goals, your budget is your GPS for money. It tells you where your money should go and helps you avoid those pesky detours. Plan for essentials like tuition, housing, and groceries, but don't forget about fun money. (Check out the worksheet for this chapter to level up your powerful money skills!)

Get Organized

Keep track of your expenses, bills, and important documents. Consider using apps or spreadsheets to stay organized. Knowing where your money goes is half the battle. Tracking your expenses helps you identify spending habits and areas where you can cut back. It's like holding up a mirror to your financial life.

Use Credit Wisely

Credit cards can be your best friend or your worst enemy. Understand how they work and use them responsibly. High-interest debt can derail your financial future.

Get a Job

Earning your own money is empowering. It not only helps with your expenses but also teaches you valuable life skills.

Don't Buy New

If you shop around for items, not only will you be able to use money saved for other essentials to enrich your life, but you'll also cultivate a thrifty attitude that will benefit many aspects of your life. Buy used textbooks and consider second-hand items. You'll save big!

Protect Yourself

Insurance may not sound exciting, but it's essential. Health, renters, and even identity theft insurance can save you from financial disasters.

Look for Ways to Spend Less

Get creative with your spending. Explore student discounts, use coupons, and look for deals. Every dollar saved adds up.

Entertain on a Budget

Having fun doesn't have to break the bank. Host movie nights, potlucks, or game nights with friends instead of pricey outings.

Stack up your savings

Based on your budget, decide how much of your paycheck you're going to add to your savings account or invest. It might be 5% or more, and every little bit can add up to seeing big dreams come true.

Tips for Saving Money

Here are 6 insider tips to help you budget like a pro and save those hard-earned earnings.

Let's dig a bit deeper into the world of healthy finances, shall we?

1. **Avoid Paying Full Price for Textbooks:** Ah, textbooks, the academic wallet vampires. But guess what? You don't always have to pay top dollar for them. Start by checking out your campus library – they might have a few copies for reference. Then, explore online resources and look for used or rental options. And hey, consider sharing with a friend or two to cut costs even further.

2. **Cook for Yourself:** Eating out every day can drain your wallet faster than you can say "fast food." If you live in an apartment, get acquainted with your kitchen, even if your culinary skills are limited to boiling water. Buy groceries and cook your meals at home. It's not only budget-friendly but also healthier. Plus, cooking can be a fun way to bond with roommates or friends. Taco Tuesdays, anyone?

3. **Embrace Communal Living:** Remember, living with others to split rent and utility costs. Plus it's not just about saving money; it's about sharing experiences and building lasting friendships. Having housemates can lead to financial savvy, fun, and an epic future. It's a win-win!

4. **Shop at Thrift Stores:** Looking stylish on a budget? Thrift stores are your fashion playground. You'll find unique, affordable clothing that won't break the bank. And hey, vintage is always in, right? Thrifting is not only trendy but also eco-friendly. Your wardrobe will thank you, and so will the planet.

5. **Use Student Discounts:** Being a student comes with perks! Flash that student ID whenever you can, and you'll be amazed at the discounts you can score. From movie tickets to tech gadgets, many places offer deals for students. Don't be shy about asking – you might just save big bucks! (Get the Most Out of Your College, 2022)

6. **Public Transportation:** Many towns offer reliable and affordable public transportation. If your town has a robust bus or subway system, it might be more cost-effective and environmentally friendly to rely on public transit rather than owning a car or using ride sharing services as your m.o.

Working Towards Financial Independence (FI)

It's important to look at a concept that can be very helpful in living life and dealing with difficulties: Financial Independence (FI). Achieving FI means having enough financial resources to support your chosen lifestyle without relying on traditional employment. It's a goal that can grant you the freedom to pursue more of your passions, make more choices that align with your values, and reduce financial stress.

Why Pursue FI?

I just can't help myself. Here's another inspiring quote, this time from Dave Ramsey: "If you will live like no one else today, later you can live like no one else."

Did reading that give you goosebumps too? FI isn't just about having a substantial bank account; it's about achieving financial freedom and security.

Here are a few reasons why pursuing FI is worth your consideration:

1. **Reduced Stress:** FI provides a safety net, reducing financial stress and allowing you to focus on personal and professional growth.

2. **Flexibility:** With FI, you have the flexibility to choose your career path, travel, or spend time on your passions without being constrained by financial obligations.

3. **Retirement Planning:** Achieving FI means you'll be better prepared for retirement, giving you the freedom to retire earlier or pursue work you're passionate about.

Side Hustles - A Way to Dip Your Toe In the Water of FI

The road to financial independence can lead to an increase in freedom and a decrease in the worries caused by financial limitations. By trying new things, having good financial habits, reading books that help you, and using powerful skills and tools, you can become more secure and free financially.

Side hustles, whether they're born of passion, necessity, the basic urge to earn money, or something else, can be a great way to start your FI journey. In Chapter 14 I've got a whole bunch of side hustle ideas to inspire you!

Keep in mind that achieving FI is a journey that requires dedication and patience, but the rewards are well worth the effort. You take the first step, and work towards the financial independence that can grant you the goals you desire.

Understanding Your Financial Situation

In the ***Chapter 12 Worksheet***, you'll get acquainted with financial terms, tips, and a handy budgeting template tool. You'll a financial superhero ready to take on the numbers and emerge victorious! So tighten your budgeting cape and get ready to experience a financial adventure.

Remember that understanding your financial situation and making wise financial choices are essential for your overall well-being. Your financial stability will influence your ability to focus on other important matters and more readily enjoy your experiences.

Now, to sum up our exploration of the financial complexities of life, let's review what we've explored. We've learned the steps to decoding your financial situation and learned a ton of thrifty tips that we can turn into powerful habits. Even fancy events like weddings won't intimidate you anymore – we talked about budgeting etiquette for those.

We gained money-mastery hacks from spending wisely to budgeting like a pro, and maybe even taking some smart steps towards FI.

In the next chapter, "Knowing Yourself & Choosing Powerful Opportunities," we touch on the importance of understanding what you want from an educational experience, the power of knowing yourself for thinking ahead to a major or career, and leveraging support from others.

Chapter 13
Knowing Yourself and Choosing Powerful Opportunities

"Self-discipline is the magic power that makes you virtually unstoppable."

-Dan Kennedy

I magine yourself standing on the brink of a new chapter in life, gazing out at the endless possibilities that education and work opportunities have to offer. Navigating a new life at a college, trade school, training program, or job is often seen as the transition to adulthood. Ready to take the plunge? It's a significant leap that promises a variety of experiences and newfound responsibilities. So, let's dig into what's in store for you and how you can create meaningful plans for your journey.

Alright, guess what? It's time for the essential disclaimer:

In these final chapters, we're going to start expanding our view and cover more topics related specifically to college, among the context of your options. Please know - It is completely, definitely, absolutely POWERFUL to understand that all of this information is food for thought. It is for those of you interested now, or later, or never! It is sustenance for your hungry questions. It is information to arm you and empower you. Why? Because in our earliest educational experiences, we hear far less about our options other than college. Yet there exist thousands and thousands of super cool, well-paying, creative, and fulfilling jobs that do not require going to college, a college degree, or setting so much as an eyeball on a college campus.

How do you find out whether you should consider going to a college or not? Courage, curiosity, and creativity. Those skills we all have. Put them to work for you!

As an example: Let's say you're thinking about becoming a doctor. Are you able to volunteer or get a part-time gig in your local clinic or hospital, to get a sneak peek into a doctor's world? Maybe you do and then you realize that you want to go into nursing. Instead of a longer educational journey, you can get your education from a community college, get to work, and feel fulfilled in your career and life. Or maybe you can't get a foot in the door. Can you get an informational interview with a doctor? I bet you can. Maybe you do, and you find out being a doctor is just what you've always dreamed of. Now, that's powerful stuff. But wait, there's more.

Interested in graphic design, carpentry, owning your own landscaping business, working in IT, childcare, data analytics, or a million other jobs? There are a multitude of ways you can get a sneak peek, or even dip your toes, into these realms of the world. And there are also many ways to get you there, without going to college.

Be brave, do research and listen to the reactions of your gut, heart, and mind. Take notes. Brainstorm ways to forge your path and emerge empowered and fulfilled. Now, not later, is when you want to start learning those powerful life skills to create your dream life.

So, as you step into this transformative phase: embrace the unknown, stay determined, and persist. In this chapter, we're diving headfirst into the exciting realm of educational choices. Each decision you make is a courageous step toward shaping your future.

It's OK To Be Figuring Out What You Want From Your Next Educational Experience

Picture your next phase of education like a blank canvas just calling for you to fill it with self-expression! Your dreams and aspirations? They're like a kaleidoscope of vibrant colors just waiting to be launched onto the canvas. Opportunities for learning are a forge where you can sculpt and mold your identity, like an artist crafting a masterpiece.

But what if you're unsure about your passions or what matters to you? It's normal and okay! Education is, after all, a journey of exploration. It's a voyage where you can explore new subjects, delve into unfamiliar theories, and discover passions you never knew existed. The key is to approach this phase with an open heart and an adventurous spirit. Be curious, be willing to embrace the unfamiliar, and most importantly, be kind to yourself as you navigate this path of discovery.

To unravel the layers of what you desire from your future years both close and far, start by exploring your values and interests. What truly matters to you? Is it personal growth, forging meaningful connections, academic excellence, or a blend of all these elements? Identifying your core values can be a powerful guide to navigating what you really want from life's choices and opportunities. (You and Your College Experience, 2012)

Understanding Your Academic Identity

Back in my early college days, I often wondered what set some students apart in terms of academic success. It wasn't just about how much they studied; it was something deeper, something I couldn't quite put my finger on. Little did I know, it was their academic identity at play.

So, what exactly is academic identity? Well, it's like the blueprint of how you view yourself as a learner. It's all about how you assess your own intelligence and how confident you feel in your role as a scholar. You see, academic identity isn't just a fancy term; it's the very core of your learning journey. (Drennan et al., 2017)

Think of it this way: Everyone possesses a unique set of things they especially value learning, and unique ways of learning, that guides their decisions, aspirations, and pursuits. Think of these values as the threads that stitch together the quilt of your identity, patching together the person you are today and the person you'd like to be tomorrow. Your educational experience, then, becomes a tapestry where these values and approaches are interwoven with every choice, every interaction, and every experience.

Now, why does defining your academic identity really matter? It matters because when you clearly understand what you value learning, and how you want to learn it, (who you are as a learner), it's like working on that quilt with a sewing machine, instead of by hand!

The Power of Knowing Yourself For Thinking Ahead to a Major or Career

Think about the possibility of being a superhero whose superpower is to have complete self-awareness. When you're empowered to feel like a worthy contributor to your own learning journey, magical things happen. You become more engaged in your classes, and you start to believe that you truly belong in those scholarly settings. Knowing your academic identity is like turning on the superhero switch that fuels your success.

At the crossroads of your academic journey lies a crucial decision that can shape your path to success: the choice of your focus of study. This decision isn't about selecting a subject you feel you *should,* or something your family expects; it's about charting a course toward your interests, goals and dreams.

As you stand on this threshold, it's important to understand that there is no one-size-fits-all approach to deciding. Instead, you can explore different approaches that resonate with your own goals and circumstances. Check it out:

The Clear Visionaries: Some individuals have possessed a clear sense of their future career path from an early age. If you find yourself in this category, your steps toward success may be more defined.

Your plan involves picking an educational program that matches your chosen career, sticking to your subject, and eventually entering your intended career or going on to more school. Your path is laser-focused, driven by a lifelong determination.

The Curious Explorers: In contrast, some enter a new school with a sense of curiosity but without a concrete career plan. You might take a diverse array of courses, savoring knowledge across various disciplines. A more definitive decision might come later in your journey when the need to specialize becomes evident. This approach allows for exploration and a genuine discovery of your passions and skills.

The Passion Pursuers: Another approach involves choosing an area of focus based on your passion for a particular subject. The goal isn't solely to secure a future career, but to immerse yourself in something you love. In the realm of college, this resonates with the essence of a liberal arts education, where personal growth and a well-rounded education take precedence. This approach prepares you for a range of career possibilities by cultivating adaptable skills.

Each of these approaches highlights the uniqueness of everyone's journeys. Your focus is not just a selection; it's a reflection of your individuality, your dreams, and your aspirations. (U.S. Department of Education, n.d.)

Keep in mind that your choice of subject isn't a final destination; it's a stepping stone toward your future. In the symphony of selecting a subject and shaping your future career, you're the composer, crafting a melody that resonates with your essence. Your focus decision isn't just a box to check; it's a step toward realizing your potential. So, go ahead and check out all the options, pick the one that fits your identity, and stride confidently forward, knowing you've got what it takes to reach the top—no matter which path you pick!

Leveraging Support in College, a Trade School or Job Training

I remember that mix of emotions like it was yesterday. I'd pack my bags with textbooks, notepads, and snacks to fuel my day. (Don't underestimate the power of those snacks!) That feeling of stepping into the unknown each day was a mixture of anticipation, excitement, and yes, a dose of fear. With so many moving parts in life to manage, doing well in school was that added stress.

But here's a tip I received that I kept top of mind to help take some pressure off myself and have a bit more courage: You don't have to do it alone. There are people who are able, and who want to help you. Teachers, counselors, mentors, coaches, you name it. They'll understand you! Because even though our paths are individual, they've all faced similar challenges and have ridden the same emotional waves. It's that understanding and support that can be your most valuable tool during these times.

So when it comes to building those supportive relationships, here are some essential nuggets of wisdom to help you prepare for this exciting voyage.

Building Relationships with Teachers

Connecting with your instructors might not seem like a time management topic, but it's an important part of optimizing your educational experience.

Introduce yourself to your teachers, outline your interests and ambitions, and you'll set the stage for a successful and enjoyable educational experience. Here's how these connections can be invaluable to your school years.

When you get to know your professors, they become guides who can help you with your academic pursuits. By letting them know about your interests and goals, you enable them to customize their advice to your individual needs, making it a more efficient and targeted approach to your studies.

They can recommend courses, books, activities, and research opportunities to help you achieve your goals. Additionally, building relationships with teachers and mentors enhances your networking skills, an essential aspect of your future career. These connections may open doors to internships, research projects, and job opportunities.

Remember, you're going to get the Adulting Treatment. Higher ed often comes with newfound freedom and responsibilities. You'll be treated as an adult, which means making decisions that impact your life and your future. Embrace this newfound agency and use it to shape your experience into a tapestry of growth and success.

So, don't hesitate to reach out to your instructors. Learning and growing isn't just about completing assignments; it's also about maximizing educational opportunities, and connecting with teachers is a great way to do that. (Willoteach, 2022)

What can you do if you feel a teacher is being unreasonable?

It's important to get along with your teachers while you're in school, but you may find yourself in a bad situation where a teacher is being unfair. Remember, these moments can be part of your academic experience, but with the right approach, you can navigate them smoothly.

First and foremost, open communication is your best tool. Approach your teacher with respect and humility to discuss your worries. Explain your perspective, and ask for theirs. Sometimes, what appears to be an unreasonable demand might stem from a misunderstanding or miscommunication.

If, after talking it through, you still think your teacher's actions are unfair, think about asking for help from other teachers or advisors you trust. They can provide a more neutral perspective and possibly mediate between you and the teacher.

I remember during my sophomore year, I found myself in a situation where I felt my literature professor was being unreasonably harsh in grading our assignments. Despite my initial frustration, I decided to seek advice from another professor I trusted. I shared my concerns, and to my surprise, they pointed out several aspects of the grading criteria which I had overlooked. This conversation not only gave me a new perspective on the situation but also encouraged me to approach my literature professor for that full dose of clarification on expectations.

Finding and Building Relationships with Counselors, Mentors & Coaches

Finding someone who is well-positioned to support you is not just about locating someone to guide you academically. True counselors, mentors and coaches provide guidance and support that nurtures your personal and professional growth alike. Here's how to know you've found one, and what working with one should, and shouldn't, look like:

Personalized Interaction: Someone who engages with you on a personal level, getting to know your interests and aspirations. They tailor their support and advice to your specific needs.

Guidance and Support: Someone who offers valuable advice and guidance based on their experiences, but only when it's relevant. They honor your unique journey - letting you find your own wisdom and ideal decisions about your educational and person goals.

Fostering Growth: A mentor's role is not only to support your day-to-day but also to encourage self-discovery and personal growth. They empower you to explore yourself and make informed decisions that will help you create the life you want.

On the other hand, here's what finding a mentor shouldn't look like:

Authoritarian Figure: Not someone who imposes their ideas on you. They should guide and support rather than dictate.

Neglecting Individuality: Not someone who tends to disregard your unique interests, goals, or identity. Instead they should respect your individuality.

Limiting Growth: Someone who you can feel stifling your independence. Their goal is to foster your growth, not restrict it. (Yousif et al., 2022)

As you prepare for this chapter of your life, don't forget that, even though you're stepping into new realms of the world, you're not alone on your journey. Just like you, lots of people are starting this journey, each with their dreams, hopes, and worries. Embrace the challenges as opportunities for growth, and seize the chance to make school a place for building strong support networks, as well as a place for learning, exploration, and making unforgettable memories.

Now it's time for the ***Chapter 13 Worksheet***, where you'll find a great tool to help you quickly set and achieve your goals. Which of your many goals will you reflect on first?

In this chapter, you've explored valuable insights. We started out by highlighting the importance of your academic identity: your values and ways of learning - those intrinsic elements that guide your decisions and aspirations. We then discussed the options of gaining support from teachers and mentors. Remember, your educational journey is a dynamic and evolving experience, and you have the tools to shape it in alignment with your vision for your life. Our identity and the mentors who support you are key. Keep asking questions, seeking guidance, and never stop pursuing your goals. And let't not forget, we completed the chapter worksheet on "How to Improve Self-Knowledge".

As we strive onward, we're now diving into the heart of "Do the Work So You Can Love Your Work". Hold onto your phone!

It's going to be a wild ride, and I know you don't want to lose that thing!

Chapter 14
Do the Work So You Can Love Your Work

"Invent your world. Surround yourself with people, color, sounds, and work that nourish you."

-Susan Ariel Rainbow Kennedy

As you consider your educational options in life, an important decision may fill your thoughts - your career goals and your first job. Setting your sights on a professional horizon might be just as important to you as acing coursework. How about we explore your career aspirations and ideas about your first job? How about some helpful tips and advice? Let's jump in.

Understanding your Career Goals

Career goals are those academic, skill and interest-based, or job-related objectives that shape your professional future. They serve as beacons of purpose, illuminating the path you'll follow to reach your career destinations. Your goals define the steps you need to take to get what you want. Setting goals early and often is powerful because they will help you make the most of your work-life journey.

But what exactly are career goals? They can be as diverse as the students themselves. Some may aspire to climb the corporate ladder in their chosen industry, while others dream of running their own businesses. Your career goals are a reflection of your interests, skills, and ambitions.

Start by envisioning your ideal day at work. What does it look like? What does your ideal work day look like in five years? Ten? Twenty? Be honest with yourself in these exercises and listen to your heart and gut, not just your brain. What do you see in your mind's eye? Write it down. Defining your interests and aspirations in this way will give you topics to research, opportunities to explore, and targets to aim for.

For instance, imagine a student who is passionate about environmental conservation. Their career goal might be to do field research, lead sustainability initiatives in a major corporation, or a thousand other things. When they set their career-related goals they can then work backwards, making changes to their study and experiential choices to become qualified candidates and effective contributors for their chosen vocation.

If your goals are still fuzzy, fret not; college is the perfect time to explore your options. Take a variety of courses, engage in extracurricular activities, and seek internships to uncover your interests. Continue taking time out to reflect on your ideal days at work, and write down what comes to mind. Over time, your goals will crystallize, and your path will become clearer.

When you've set your sights on a career path, the next question arises: What do you want from a first job? The choices are vast, so understanding your desires and handling diverse job offerings and challenges is essential. (Career Goals for College Students, 2022)

Understand what you want from a job

Your first job after college is a significant milestone, but it's essential to approach it with a clear understanding of your expectations. While it might not be your dream job right out of the gate, your initial employment should align with your long-term career goals.

Think about whether your first job helps you learn skills and experience you'll use later in your career. Think of it as a stepping stone that helps you build the foundation necessary for your future success.

If you encounter challenges or goals that don't match your expectations, use them as opportunities to define your career path further. Seek mentorship and guidance from experienced professionals to help you make informed decisions and overcome obstacles.

Your first job is a valuable stepping stone that contributes to your overall professional journey. Embrace it as part of your ongoing learning process, and stay focused on your long-term career goals. With dedication, resilience, and adaptability, you can pave the way to a successful and fulfilling career. (Stewart et al., 2019)

Why is it important to set work and career goals?

As a college student, you might feel like you're at a crossroads in life, with lots of possibilities and potential futures. In this pivotal moment, setting clear goals becomes a compass guiding you through the exciting yet uncertain journey of higher education. Let's delve into the reasons why goal-setting is paramount for college students.

Creating a defined career path

Imagine embarking on a long road trip without a destination in mind; you might end up lost and disoriented. Goals act as your career GPS, helping you chart a defined path. They provide clarity, focus, and purpose, steering you toward a career that aligns with your aspirations.

Establishing educational needs

College is not just about attending classes; it's about equipping yourself with the knowledge and skills needed for your future career. Setting educational goals helps you identify the courses, majors, or activities that will help you become an expert in your field.

Establishing important relationships

Your college years offer a unique opportunity to build a valuable network of mentors, peers, and industry professionals. Setting goals to establish meaningful relationships can open doors to internships, research collaborations, and job opportunities. Building these connections can be as essential as your formal education.

Improving specific industry skills

Setting goals to enhance specific industry-related skills can give you a significant advantage. To become a desirable candidate, target specific skills like programming, data analysis, and communication. (Career Goals for College Students, 2022)

7 Career Goals and Strategies

1. **Master a specific industry specialization or skill**: Setting a goal to master a particular specialization or skill relevant to your chosen career can be a game-changer. It shows your dedication to becoming an expert in your field.

2. **Achieve top grades to attract better job offers**: High grades can open doors to more job opportunities and competitive job offers. Striving for excellence in your coursework is a worthy goal.

3. **Develop a strong professional network**: Networking is an essential part of building your career. Setting a goal to establish connections with professionals in your field can lead to internships, mentorship, and job referrals.

4. **Strive to achieve the salary you want**: If financial stability is crucial for you, setting a salary goal can guide your job search and negotiation process.

5. **Find an internship in your desired industry**: Internships offer hands-on experience and a chance to explore your chosen field. Setting a goal to secure internships can bridge the gap between classroom learning and real-world application.

6. **Gain additional certifications or educational credentials:** To stand out in competitive industries, additional certifications or educational credentials can be invaluable. Setting goals to earn these qualifications will enhance your resume.

7. **Work for a specific company or organization:** If you have a dream company or organization in mind, setting a goal to

work for them can be a motivating force. (Setting Different Types of Career Goals, 2023)

By setting and pursuing career goals, you can transform your skills into a launching pad for future success. These goals provide direction, purpose, and motivation, ultimately propelling you toward your dream career. So, as you navigate your educational options, remember that setting clear goals is not just a choice; it's a powerful strategy for building your dream future.

Next up: Side Hustles. I've seen students embark on remarkable journeys of entrepreneurship alongside their studies.

Striving for Side Hustle Success

One of the most effective ways to work towards financial independence is by exploring side hustles. These additional income streams can be a game-changer. Here are some side hustle ideas to consider:

1. **Freelancing:** Leverage your skills and expertise to offer freelance services in areas such as data entry, web design, social media management and content writing.

2. **Online Selling:** Start an e-commerce store on platforms like Etsy or eBay, selling handmade crafts, vintage items, or unique products.

3. **Tutoring:** If you excel in a particular subject or skill, consider offering tutoring services to students in need of academic support.

4. **Content Creation:** If you're passionate about a topic, start a

blog, YouTube channel, or podcast and monetize it through advertising, sponsorships, or merchandise sales.

5. **Sell Pre-Loved Items**: Declutter your space and make money by selling items you no longer need online or at garage sales.

6. **Sell Baked Goods**: If you're a whiz in the kitchen, turn your passion for baking into a side hustle. Sell your delicious treats to friends and peers, or at local markets.

7. **Babysitting**: Babysitting is a classic side hustle. If you enjoy spending time with children, it can be a rewarding and lucrative option.

8. **Dog Walker:** Love dogs? Become a dog walker or pet sitter in your spare time. It's a fun way to earn extra cash.

9. **Food Delivery**: With the rise of food delivery apps, becoming a food courier can be a flexible and profitable gig.

10. **Landscaping Crew:** If you're comfortable with lawn and garden equipment, can work outdoors rain or shine and enjoy making money, this could be a perfect gig.

11. **Service Crew**: Working in restaurants or cafes can provide you with valuable customer service experience and tips. (Engel, 2023)

When considering these side hustles, keep in mind that your choice should align with your skills, interests, and schedule. These opportunities can take place along your chosen path, teaching you valuable lessons about entrepreneurship, time management, customer service, and even lead you to financial independence.

For those jobs where you'll be interacting with others (*99% of jobs one way or another*), you'll need to develop your skills in effective communication.

Effective Communication in the Workplace

Effective communication in the workplace is an essential skill that can make or break your experiences. It's a vital tool for creating a productive and harmonious work environment. In this section, we will explore various strategies to enhance your communication effectiveness. (Pro tip: These strategies can be effective in your personal life, too!)

Set Clear Goals and Expectations: Communication thrives on clarity. When you establish clear goals and expectations, your team knows what to aim for. Ambiguity can lead to misunderstandings and inefficiencies. It's like giving your travel buddies a roadmap with the destination circled, plus step-by-step directions; they'll know the destination and, even better, how to get there.

Ask Clarifying Questions: The art of asking questions cannot be underestimated. It demonstrates your commitment to understanding and your willingness to engage in a conversation. If you're unsure about something, don't hesitate to ask for clarification. It will save time, prevent misunderstandings, and foster better relationships.

Schedule Regular One-on-One Meetings: One-on-one meetings are an excellent way to build strong working relationships. They provide a dedicated space for open dialogue. It's a time for discussing concerns, sharing feedback, and aligning on goals. These meetings can be invaluable for understanding your team's needs and fostering a supportive work environment.

Praise in Public, Criticize in Private: Public recognition can boost morale and motivate your team. When someone excels, acknowledge it in front of their peers. On the flip side, if criticism is necessary, do it in private. Nobody benefits from being criticized in front of their colleagues. Private discussions can be more constructive and less embarrassing.

Assume Positive Intent: This is a golden rule of communication. Always assume that your colleagues have positive intentions. If someone's words or actions are unclear, it's often due to miscommunication, not malice. This assumption can lead to more amicable interactions.

Repeat Important Messages: Repetition can be a powerful tool for reinforcing essential messages. If there's a critical piece of information or a key objective, don't hesitate to repeat it. This redundancy ensures that everyone is on the same page and reduces the chances of critical information being missed.

Raise Your Words, Not Your Voice: Yelling doesn't equate effective communication. In fact, it can harm relationships and create a hostile work environment. Instead of raising your voice, focus on raising the clarity and intention of your words. Speak confidently but respectfully, maintaining control of the situation.

Likewise, if someone else begins to raise their voice, listen actively. "Read the room." Come to understand when someone is upset, whether to continue engaging, or disengage from the conversation. Remember, there is something to be learned from a conflict, just as with every other interaction.

Town Hall Meetings and Cross-Functional Check-Ins: Larger meetings, such as town halls, provide an opportunity for disseminating important information and fostering a sense of unity within the organization. Cross-functional check-ins ensure that different departments collaborate effectively. Pay attention in these meetings, ask questions and offer any unique insights you may have into your work. (Effective Communication in the Workplace, n.d.)

Now it's time to complete the final TWO worksheets! In the first, you'll reflect on your passions, strengths, weaknesses. (Weaknesses aren't bad - they're just the opposite of your strengths. One fact of life is balance, after all.) In the second, you'll be prompted to give some serious consideration to your educational options. Complete the ***Chapter 14 Worksheets.***

Time for a recap! This chapter got us thinking about how we need to do some work now, so that we can love the work we're doing later. We established the practicality of thinking and planning ahead in terms of a major and career.

The "7 Career Goals & Strategies" section served as a navigator, illuminating the diverse goals that students can set. We reflected on why it's important to establish work and career goals, considered that big list of side hustle ideas, and wrapped up with a thought-provoking section on how to communicate effectively at work. Last but not least, we completed the chapter worksheet on "Creating Goals for Your Educational Experience".

Now, let's pivot to our next chapter where we'll explore "Options To Accelerate A College Education." Are you already on board with using powerful life skills? Do you already like saving time and money? Get excited for this one!

Chapter 15
Options For Accelerating A College Education

"You don't get what you wish for. You get what you work for."

-Daniel Milstein

Alright, so we're about to unearth two particularly powerful ways you can alter the course of your educational journey.

When you're navigating the high school landscape, you'll likely encounter the options of honors and Advanced Placement (AP) classes. Understanding the distinctions between these two types of courses can significantly impact your academic journey, especially if you choose to go to college. Simply put, taking certain courses can: 1. Improve your future college prospects and 2. Accelerate your education by earning you college credit before you even attend.

But what about after high school? That where CLEP exams enter the scene. These tests are all about getting college credit for stuff you already know, or can learn by studying up. These tests can: 1. Accelerate your education by earning you college credit outside of courses and 2. Save you hundreds or thousands by bypassing the need for some college courses.

Let's do this thing!

What Are the Differences Between Honors and AP Classes?

Honors classes and AP classes offer enriched educational experiences, but they differ in several key aspects. Honors classes delve deeply into standard course material, providing greater insight and more challenging content than regular classes. This increased rigor translates into more extended study hours, demanding projects, and challenging tests.

On the other hand, AP classes, standing for Advanced Placement, offer an introduction to college-level coursework. The critical distinction lies in the possibility of earning college credit by achieving high scores on corresponding AP exams. These classes are demanding, requiring extensive after-school studying, and culminate with comprehensive exams. Some colleges grant credit for scores of 3 and above, while more elite institutions may only recognize scores of 4 or 5. (Honors vs. AP Classes, 2021)

To make an informed decision about whether to enroll in honors or AP courses, you must understand their distinctions, including:

Ability to Earn College Credit: AP classes offer the potential to earn college credit, whereas honors courses typically do not.

Difficulty Level: AP classes are more challenging than honors courses due to their college-level curriculum and demanding exams.

Class Availability: Honors classes may be more accessible and offered in a broader range of subjects compared to AP classes.

GPA Weight: AP classes often carry a higher GPA weight than honors classes. (Epps, 2021)

When deciding between honors and AP classes, consider your educational goals. If you want to get college credits, focus on AP classes in your best subjects and take honors or regular classes in the other ones. But if you're trying to get into a super selective college, a mix of AP and honors classes can boost your GPA and make your academic record look better. (Honors College. 2023)

What Are CLEP Exams and What Are the Benefits?

In addition to your high school coursework, you may have the opportunity to earn college credit through the College-Level Examination Program (CLEP) exams. These exams are multiple-choice and created by college professors. The questions are based on material typically taught in lower-level college courses, and each test typically takes between 90 to 120 minutes to complete. CLEP offers 34 different tests across a wide range of subjects, making it a versatile option for students. Following the exam, you'll receive your scores instantly, except for exams with a writing section. Check with your college's Advising Office to find out if your college accepts CLEP credits toward your degree. (Claybourn, 2023)

Choosing Which Exams to Take

The decision of which CLEP exams to undertake hinges on several critical factors. The following questions will aid you in making an informed choice:

School Acceptance: Determine which CLEP exams are recognized by your educational institution.

Minimum Score: Discover the minimum score required by your school to grant credit for each exam.

Credit Awards: Evaluate how many credits your school awards for each CLEP exam, ensuring it aligns with your academic aspirations.

Maximum Credit Hours: Be aware of the maximum number of credit hours you can earn through CLEP exams, ensuring you navigate this academic landscape with precision. (Coursera. 2023)

How to Register for CLEP Exams

By registering for CLEP exams, you take control of your education. Here are the steps for taking exams:

Choose the Exam: Begin your journey by selecting the CLEP exam that aligns with your academic pursuits and expertise.

Create a CLEP Account: Whether signing in to your existing CLEP account or setting up a new one, your account will be your gateway to the CLEP exams world.

Select Test Center and Score Reporting: Choose your test center and where you want your score report sent to ensure your achievements are recorded correctly.

Schedule Your Exam: Use the test center search tool to book a convenient exam time that seamlessly integrates with your study schedule. (Coursera, 2023)

Within this chapter, you've gained essential insights into academic choices, spanning Honors and AP classes to the versatile CLEP exams.

As you continue your education, check in with yourself about your work and life aspirations, and make your goal to manage the balance between classes, extracurriculars, and life outside of school. How do you want to spend your time and money? What are you working toward?

You've got this!

Chapter 16
College Planning 101

"Work hard, nap hard."

-*Demi Lovato*

When I started my college journey, I didn't fully grasp that it wouldn't be just another pitstop in life. It turns out that college is like a magical chrysalis, where you get the chance to transform into the person you've always dreamt of becoming. I didn't realize either, just how much I'd grow accustomed to napping - but hey if it works for caterpillars, who was I to judge?

Starting college isn't just about showing up on campus; it's about exploring yourself, growing, and opening up a world of possibilities. Take a moment to pause and reflect on why you are at this juncture, which things are of importance to you, and what you are expecting to gain from this journey. This is a great time to reconsider your goals and confirm your enthusiasm for them as you explore your college options.

What lies at the heart of your college experience isn't just a degree-it's the ultimate hunt for self-discovery. It's the chance to uncover your passions, and blaze a trail in the world! To truly understand what you want from your college experience, it's essential to embark on an introspective journey. Begin by reflecting on your values – the principles that guide your choices and shape your perspective. What matters to you most? Is it knowledge, creativity, social impact, personal growth, or perhaps a blend of these elements? (Evans, 2022)

Now, choosing the right college might sound like a daunting task, but let me assure you, it can be an exciting ride filled with choices, opportunities, and growth. So, grab your notepad and pen, tablet, or whatever you prefer. Let's navigate this together!

College Options

First off, let's talk about YOU. Yeah, you! What do you expect from your college experience? You've got the choice of small class sizes and a close community, tons of resources at a big school, or a specialized program that suits your interests.

Exploring Community, State (Public), and Private Colleges

Let's dive into one of the biggest decisions – between three types colleges. It's like picking between three epic concerts, each with its unique vibe, that'll rock your academic world.

I faced the same choice, each had its attractions, and I had to weigh the pros and cons. Ultimately, my decision shaped not just my education but also my overall college experience. It's a decision that sets the stage for your academic adventure.

When beginning my college experience, I began to evaluate the advantages and disadvantages of attending a community college, a 4-year state university, or a 4-year private institution as if I were comparing the features of three different phones. Each of them had its special charm, like the three leading institutes of education.

Community colleges are known for their cost-effective approach to education, providing an affordable starting point for your academic journey. Most of these offer 2-year programs that lead to an Associate's degree. Most of them also offer a greater variety of specialized training programs that lead to degrees in Social Work, Nursing, EMT training, Automotive, and Computer Science, to name a few. Choosing one of these programs can be a fabulous way to get the exact training you want and get working right away!

Since I had done the work to decide I wanted to go for a Bachelor's degree, the route I took was to take as many "Gen Eds" and electives as I could, so that I could transfer the credits to a 4-year school. Because my program was more flexible, I could also choose to take a part-time or full-time course load, from one semester to the next. This allowed me to dip my toes into college courses without committing to a much bigger price tag, or a strict full-time program.

State schools strike a balance between affordability and a wider range of program offerings. What's the scoop? In-state students get a discount on tuition – it's like getting a government subsidy for your education! They offer a smorgasbord of academic programs and usually have a bustling student population. If you're in-state, you're in luck because tuition is often lower for you. State schools can also be your ticket to some incredible research opportunities, especially if your interests match up with your state's industries or initiatives. Financial aid is in the mix too, and guess what? Public colleges often roll out the welcome mat for in-state applicants.

Private colleges usually offer even more specialized courses, smaller class sizes, and networking opportunities that can enhance your professional prospects. (Epps, 2021) You can imagine private colleges as the exclusive VIP parties of the college world. They're funded by tuition, endowments, and private donations. This means higher tuition fees. But hey, don't fret, because some private colleges dish out generous financial aid packages as well. Plus, they often serve up specialized programs that are like finding rare vinyl in a record store. And if you're into unique extracurricular activities and networking opportunities, private colleges can prove their value as well. (Epps, 2020)

Regarding cost, you've got to weigh the tuition fees against potential financial aid and scholarships. Meanwhile, State schools often have deep pockets thanks to government funding. Your decision in choosing between the two depends on your style, financial situation, and academic goals. So, think it through, weigh those pros and cons, and make a call that'll put you on the path to college stardom!

Moving on, let's channel your growth into the next part of this chapter, Crafting Your College Application Strategy. This step will be a vital part of your journey as you aim to shape your future and reach your academic and career goals.

Crafting Your College Application Strategy

A key question arises: How many colleges should you apply to? Admissions experts advise applying to a range of four to twelve schools, based on your budget for application fees. This approach allows you to create a balanced application strategy.

First up, are the "reach" schools. These are the rockstars of colleges, the ones you've been daydreaming about. They might feel like you're reaching for the stars, but hey, you've got a shot!

Then, the "target" schools. The type that fit you like a glove. You've got a good chance of getting in, and they're right up your alley.

Now, let's not forget about the "safety" schools. These are like that comfort playlist you turn to when you need a pick-me-up. They'll welcome you with open arms, no doubt about it.

Your College Checklist

Alright, picture this: You're on the lookout to find the perfect college, and it's like assembling your dream playlist. You're the DJ, and these factors are your hit tracks for an unforgettable college experience.

Learning Environment: Do you thrive in intimate, interactive classrooms or enjoy the energy of a packed lecture hall? Private colleges are like those exclusive gigs with smaller class sizes, while public colleges might offer a mix of large and small classes. It's all about what amps up your educational experience.

Campus Life: Your college campus is your second home, so let's talk about the vibes. Check out the extracurricular activities, clubs, and organizations each college offers. Are there cool opportunities that match your interests and passions? Campus life is where you'll make lifelong connections and grow personally. Dive into campus culture through online resources and visits to ensure it jives with your values.

Campus Diversity: Diversity is like the remix that makes your college experience pop. It exposes you to different perspectives and cultures. Whether it's a private or public college, look into cultural organizations, events, and inclusivity initiatives. A diverse campus creates a vibrant learning environment that gets you ready for a globalized world.

Class Size: Let's talk class sizes – your front-row seats to learning. Smaller classes, like those at private colleges, mean more personalized attention and active participation. Public colleges offer options too, with a mix of large lectures and cozy discussion sections. It's all about your learning style and how much one-on-one time you need.

Athletics and Extracurriculars: College is your stage, and these are your supporting acts. If you're into sports or specific extracurricular activities, check out what each college offers. Division I schools bring the sports heat, while Division III schools balance academics and athletics. Plus, there are clubs, arts groups, and community service opportunities that make your college journey a hit (Ngo, 2020)

As you go through college, you'll come across lots of chances and decisions that can really boost your learning and help you grow. Some of the most significant decisions you might make are whether to study abroad, pursue an internship, engage in extracurricular activities, or volunteer. These experiences can shape your college years and provide valuable insights into your future. Let's explore each of these choices to help you decide if they're right for you. (WikiHow, 2023)

Study Abroad: How to Decide if Study Abroad is Right for You

Studying abroad can be a life-changing experience, exposing you to different cultures and perspectives while expanding your academic horizons. To decide if it's right for you, consider your goals, both academically and personally. Ask yourself:

Academic Objectives: Are there courses or programs abroad that align with your major or interests? Studying abroad can be a fantastic opportunity to gain a global perspective on your field of study.

Personal Growth: Are you open to new experiences, cultural differences, and stepping out of your comfort zone? Adaptability and a willingness to embrace change are crucial for a successful study abroad adventure.

Financial Considerations: Assess the costs and funding options. Explore scholarships and financial aid opportunities. If finances are a concern, it's essential to plan and budget effectively.

Duration: Decide whether a short-term program or a full semester/year is a better fit for your academic goals and personal preferences. (Great Learning, 2023)

Internships: How to Decide if an Internship is Right for You

Internships provide hands-on experience in your chosen field and can significantly impact your career trajectory. Here's how to decide if an internship is right for you:

Career Goals: Consider your long-term career objectives. If your field values practical experience, internships are often the bridge between academics and your dream job.

Networking: Internships offer the chance to connect with professionals in your field. Evaluate the potential connections you can make during your internship.

Academic Balance: Ensure your academic responsibilities can co-exist with your internship. Balancing both effectively requires strong time management skills.

Compensation: Decide whether you're willing to accept unpaid internships or if you need financial compensation. Both options have their pros and cons. (Resources. 2020)

Extracurricular Activities: Emphasis on the "Extra"

Extracurricular activities offer opportunities to explore your interests outside the classroom. Here's how to decide when to participate:

Balance: Avoid overloading your schedule with too many activities. While they can enhance your resume, too many commitments can lead to burnout and negatively affect your academic performance.

Relevance: Engage in activities that genuinely interest you or align with your career goals. Avoid joining clubs or organizations just to pad your resume.

Quality Over Quantity: One or two meaningful extracurricular activities where you actively contribute or lead can have a more significant impact than being a passive member of many groups.

Passion Projects: Pursue passion projects or start your own clubs if you can't find an existing organization that matches your interests. (Swain, 2019)

On-Campus vs Off-Campus Jobs

On the journey through the academic maze, college life often comes with the added challenge of managing finances. It's a delicate balancing act, and one way students navigate this is by taking on part-time jobs. Whether you choose to work on-campus or venture into off-campus employment, it's a significant decision that can shape your college experience in unique ways. So, let's embark on an exploration of the benefits, pros, and cons of on-campus versus off-campus jobs.

Benefits

Imagine a college student's life – textbooks, lectures, exams, and a constant struggle to optimize a finite amount of time. Amid this hustle, some students take the bold step of working part-time during the school year. Surprisingly, research suggests that these students tend to perform better academically than those who don't. It's like the act of balancing work and study hones their focus, organization, and time management skills.

Not only that, but earning cash while in school creates more opportunities for you both in the present and in the future. Whether it's saving to pay off your student loan debt, saving for a car or home, or just paying your daily expenses, cash earned in the present affords you chances to put it to work for you. Practice using it, understand its true value in your life now, and learn about its potential value to you in the future.

Now, let's dive into the heart of the matter: the options for student employment. You have two broad choices – on and off-campus jobs. (Williams, 2022)

On-Campus Jobs

Pros:

- Flexible Schedules: On-campus positions often offer more flexible work hours that can be adjusted to suit your class schedule. These jobs understand your academic commitments.

- Easier Access and Proximity: You don't need to commute far or deal with the logistics of off-campus employment. Your workplace is right within the college premises.

Cons:

- Your on-campus job paychecks may go to tuition and fees, leaving you with less for personal expenses. This could be a downside for some more than others.

- Lower Rates of Pay: Typically, on-campus jobs pay lower hourly rates compared to some off-campus opportunities, which may affect your overall income.

Off-Campus Jobs

Pros:

- Potential for Better Income: With off-campus work, you might have access to a wider array of job opportunities that pay more. This extra income could ease financial burdens.

- Real-World Exposure: These jobs offer a taste of the 'real world.' The experience gained may contribute positively to your resume, making you more marketable post-graduation.

Cons:

- Transportation Issues: Off-campus jobs might require commuting, and you'll need to factor in transportation costs, which can eat into your earnings.

- Less Flexibility: Many off-campus jobs demand full shifts, which can be more demanding and less flexible when compared to the tailored schedules of on-campus positions.

As you stand at the crossroads of on-campus and off-campus job choices, remember that there's no one-size-fits-all answer. Your decision should align with your goals, priorities, and the level of financial responsibility you're willing to shoulder. So, weigh your options, consider your financial situation, and take the path that best suits your college journey. Campus offices and off-campus businesses will have an impact on your college experience, adding depth and breadth to your life.

Volunteering: When to Participate, When Not To

Volunteering is a noble endeavor but must be approached thoughtfully. Here's how to decide when to participate:

Motivation: Examine your reasons for volunteering. If it's solely to bolster your resume, reconsider your motives. Authentic passion for the cause makes for a more fulfilling experience.

Time Management: Ensure volunteering doesn't compromise your academic performance or other commitments. Set clear boundaries and allocate time wisely.

Long-Term Commitment: Long-term volunteering commitments can be more impactful for both you and the organization you're helping. Short-term projects might not offer the same depth of experience. That's not a reason not to volunteer short-term, but it's worth bearing in mind that each option may have different effects on what you take away from the experiences.

Diversity of Experience: While consistency is valuable, diversifying your volunteering experiences may help you gain a broader range of skills and perspectives.

Now, let's rewind a bit and talk about what we've been up to in this chapter.

We've been on a thrilling ride, exploring college options and making informed decisions. We tackled the nitty-gritty differences between community, state, and private colleges, considering stuff like costs, what they offer, and research opportunities. Research opportunities are wide– sometimes colleges have in-depth research or niche opportunities. Some private colleges are like headlining acts in specific fields.

Careful consideration of each opportunity's potential benefits and your own interests will help you make choices that enrich your college experience and set you on a path to a successful future. (Lindoph, 2020) Use these insights and strategies as a compass to steer your academic voyage with confidence. How you choose to study abroad, get involved in internships, or volunteer is crucial to your academic success.

As we wrap up this final chapter of "Powerful Life Skills", it's time to bring our discussion to a close. We've covered an array of essential topics, and equipped you with knowledge, insights, skills and strategies to practice that will empower you in your education, work, and every other aspect of life.

Your young adult years are only the beginning of a remarkable life filled with growth and self-discovery. As you embrace your future, apply the knowledge and skills you've acquired throughout this book, and stay committed to lifelong learning.

Create Your Dream Life

As we reach the culmination of this guide, it's time to take a step back and appreciate the remarkable journey you've been on—the journey towards your living dream life. This journey has been filled with unexpected twists and turns, but through it all, you've remained committed to your goals and ambitions. You've learned a lot and grown as a person, and you're now ready to take on the next phase of your life.

Throughout the chapters, you've gained insights, strategies, advice and powerful skills to navigate the many facets of your school life, work life, and personal life. The real heart of my wish for you is in taking the time to savor every instant, the struggles, the successes, and the priceless lessons that will develop you into the individual you are meant to be.

If I could capture the spirit of this book in a few words, it would be about empowerment, resilience, and embracing the extraordinary journey of designing your life. It's not merely about academic pursuits; it's a profound exploration of your true self. Here, you've embarked on a transformative experience, one that bears testament to your courage and your boundless potential.

Moving Forward with Confidence

First and foremost, "Powerful Life Skills" is a reminder that your journey is unique, and there is no one-size-fits-all formula for success. It's about understanding your individuality and embracing your authenticity. It's about having the courage to explore uncharted territories within yourself, to challenge your own limits with curiosity, and to leverage your creativity to nurture your self-awareness.

It's also about the importance of self-care and self-love. Remember that taking care of your well-being, both physically and mentally, is not a luxury but a necessity. Love and respect yourself throughout this journey, and you'll find that your capacity for love and empathy towards others will grow.

Support is another crucial element. In school and in life, we all need a helping hand from time to time. Don't hesitate to reach out to your friends, family, mentors, coaches, counselors, and support networks. Their guidance, encouragement, and understanding are your most valuable assets.

Lifelong learning is a cornerstone of becoming an awesome and powerful adult. Recognize that your education doesn't stop with a degree or certificate. Every day, every experience, and every challenge is an opportunity to learn and grow. Stay curious, stay hungry for knowledge, and you'll find the world is an endless source of inspiration.

Preparing for Post-School Life

As you approach the final chapters of any educational journey, it's natural to think about what's next. The transition from one educational experience to another life situation can be both exhilarating and daunting. But remember that you're more prepared and powerful than you think.

The skills you'll acquire throughout your school years are not just for exams and assignments. They are tools you'll use in your career, your personal life, and in contributing to the world. So, approach the future with confidence. You'll hone your time management, critical thinking, communication, research, and problem-solving abilities. You'll learn how to build relationships and connect with mentors. All of this will serve you well in the professional world and beyond.

Furthermore, you'll gain a profound understanding of diversity, empathy, and the power of self-identity. These lessons are invaluable in forging meaningful relationships and creating your fulfilling dream life. Continue to embrace diversity, practice empathy, and respect the experiences and perspectives of others. These skills, along with the powerful three, will set you apart.

Final Thoughts and Inspirational Messages for the Journey Ahead

As this guidebook draws to a close, I wish to make sure that you depart with a feeling of enthusiasm and a strong sense of resolve. Your positive mindset, dreams and skills will kick off a life-changing journey that can unlock your aspirations and a powerful future. Welcome the thrilling experience of your powerful dream life with an eager spirit.

I intended for this book to be more than just a young-adulting companion; it's a life companion. The pursuit of knowledge and personal growth is not limited to your earliest school years; it's a lifelong endeavor. Continue to challenge yourself, push boundaries, and resist the allure of comfort with mediocrity. Always set new goals and reach for greater heights. Not for any other reason than to do things that make you feel fulfilled.

In addition to the invaluable insights contained within these pages, I encourage you to reflect on your learnings regularly. Share your thoughts, experiences, and newfound wisdom with others. Writing notes, reflections, and ideas throughout your journey can help solidify your understanding while inspiring fellow travelers to embark on their own path to their powerful dream life.

Most importantly, nurture your self-belief. Recognize that you possess far more capabilities than you may presently realize. Your potential is boundless, and your dreams are worthy of pursuit. Forge ahead with true confidence, making your school years and the years beyond truly rewarding. You wield the power to craft the life you desire, and I wholeheartedly believe in your ability to do so.

Now and always, embrace your journey, for you are the author of your unique and extraordinary story. Your experiences, your choices, and your passions will shape this narrative full of infinite potential. Seize the pen with gusto and write each chapter with intention and enthusiasm. Create your dream life as you would write it on a page!

~~~~~~~
~~~~~~~

If you've found this book to be a valuable resource, I kindly ask you to consider leaving a review. Sharing your experience and insights can serve as a guiding light for others as they embark on their own path towards their dream lives. Your review has the potential to make a significant impact on one or many, offering support and wisdom when it's needed most. Both the QR code below and following link will bring you to this book's Amazon.com page where you can leave a review: https://amzn.to/3GtAHkx

Remember, your words have the power to inspire, encourage, and change lives. Thank you for being part of this world, and for paying it forward with your voice!

About the Author

Lindsey Goodwin is a life coach, author, artist and avid traveler. Her life coaching business, *Infinite Futures Coaching*, was born from a seed planted during her early work and educational years in Massachusetts. She now lives near Galveston, Texas and loves supporting people to practice powerful skills, grow to be empowered, and create lives they love. Learn more at https://www.infinitefuturescoaching.com.

References

10 Tips for Healthy Relationships in College. (n.d.). SUU. https://www.suu.edu/blog/2018/08/ten-tips-for-healthy-relationships.html

10 Tips for Living with a Roommate. (n.d.). UWYO. https://www.uwyo.edu/admissions/blog/2020/campus/roommate-tips.html

14 Creative Ways to Engage Students. (n.d.). Center for Excellence in Learning and Teaching. https://www.celt.iastate.edu/instructional-strategies/teaching-format/14-creative-ways-to-engage-students/

30 Side Hustles Perfect for College Students. (2018). Great Value Colleges. https://www.greatvaluecolleges.net/side-hustles-for-college-students/

4 Ways to Avoid Being a Victim of an Unfair Teacher. (n.d.). WikiHow. https://www.wikihow.com/Avoid-Being-a-Victim-of-an-Unfair-Teacher

7 Examples of Career Goals for College Students. (2022). Indeed Career Guide. https://www.indeed.com/career-advice/career-development/career-goals-for-college-students

7 Fitness Apps For Your Best Workout From Anywhere. (2020, March 29). Hilton Grand Vacations. https://www.hiltongrandvacations.com/en/plan-your-vacation/travel-tips/7-free-fitness-apps-for-your-best-workout-from-anywhere

7 Time Management Tools to Increase Your Productivity - Revolution Learning and Development Ltd. (2021, August 9). Www.revolutionlearning.co.uk. https://www.revolutionlearning.co.uk/blog/7-time-management-tools/

8 Self-Care Tips To Manage Stress. (2013, November 24). Psych Central. https://psychcentral.com/stress/practicing-self-care-during-stressful-times

8 Ways to Get the Most Out of Your College Experience | U.S. Department of Education. (n.d.). Www.ed.gov. https://www.ed.gov/content/8-ways-get-most-out-your-college-experience

Amherst College. (2006). 10 Tips for Healthy Relationships | Healthy Relationships | Amherst College. Www.amherst.edu. https://www.amherst.edu/campuslife/health-safety-wellness/counseling/self_care/healthy_relationships/10_tips_for_health_relationships

A Student's Guide to Buying a Car in College. (n.d.). Www.pnc.com. https://www.pnc.com/insights/personal-finance/spend/buying-a-car-in-college.html

Auld, S. (2019, November 10). Critical thinking: an essential skill for

every student. ACC Blog. https://www.acc.edu.au/blog/critical-thi
nking-essential-skill/

Barbara L. Fredrickson, Ph.D. | Authentic Happiness. (2013). Up
enn.edu. https://www.authentichappiness.sas.upenn.edu/faculty-p
rofile/barbara-l-fredrickson-phd

BestColleges.com. BestColleges.com; BestColleges.com. https://
www.bestcolleges.com/resources/balancing-stress/

Bobby Rae (August 3, 2023). Benefits of a digital calendar: Saving
time in the workplace. Doodle.com. https://doodle.com/en/benefit
s-of-a-digital-calendar-saving-time-in-the-workplace/

Bortz, D. (2018, August 21). The College Student's Guide to Find-
ing a Great Apartment. Real Estate News & Insights | Realtor.c
om®. https://www.realtor.com/advice/rent/college-student-find-gr
eat-apartment/

Buy & Sell Cars: Reviews, Prices, and Financing - CarGurus. (n.d.).
Www.cargurus.com. Retrieved October 27, 2023, from
https://www.cargurus.com/?gclid=CjwKCAjwnOipBhBQEiwACy
GLuo0IZ34gLAc-_ojEqyFqQzq5REzEn6vv6QxdAsIxl_T928DJp
QOz5hoCKI8QAvD_BwE

Carvana | Buy & Finance Used Cars Online | Skip The Dealership.
(2019). https://www.carvana.com

Clarke, M., Drennan, J., Hyde, A., & Politis, Y. (2018). The impact of austerity on Irish higher education faculty. Higher Education, 75, 1047-1060.

Claybourn, C. (2023, March 14). CLEP exams: what to know. US News & World Report. https://www.usnews.com/education/best-colleges/articles/clep-exams-what-to-know

College Dorm Life: What to Expect Your First Year on Campus. (n.d.). Fastweb. https://www.fastweb.com/student-news/articles/college-dorm-life-what-to-expect-your-first-year-on-campus

College Success | SUNY OER Services (2018, October 3). https://oer.suny.edu/courses/college-success

Coping with Peer Pressure: Building Resilience & Self-Confidence | Therapy for Young Adults | Therapy for Colorado (n.d.). Two Rivers Therapy & Consulting.
https://www.tworiverstherapycolorado.com/blog/coping-with-peer-pressure-strategies-for-building-resilience-and-self-confidence

Coursera (2023, February 16). What is effective communication? Skills for work, school, and life. Coursera. https://www.coursera.org/articles/communication-effectiveness

Creative Thinking Skills | College Success. (2012). Lumenlearning.com. https://courses.lumenlearning.com/suny-collegesuccess-lumen1/chapter/creative-thinking-skills/

Effective Communication in the Workplace (n.d.). Extension.psu.edu. Retrieved October 26, 2023, from https://extension.psu.edu/effective-communication-in-the-workplace#:~:text=Listen%20more%20than%20talk.

Engel, I. (2023, May 20). 6 of the best side hustles for college students—some pay over $30 per hour. CNBC. https://www.cnbc.com/2023/05/20/best-side-hustles-for-college-students.html

Epps, T. (2020, December 1). Private vs. Public Colleges: Key Differences | BestColleges. BestColleges.com. https://www.bestcolleges.com/blog/private-vs-public-colleges/

Epps, T. (2021, February 14). Private vs. Public Colleges: What's the Difference? | BestColleges. Www.bestcolleges.com. https://www.bestcolleges.com/blog/private-vs-public-colleges/

Evans, E. (2022, March 17). Understanding what's important to college students. Qualtrics. https://www.qualtrics.com/blog/college-experience

Falcon, L. (2015, June). Breaking Down Barriers: First-Generation College Students and College Success | The League for Innovation in the Community College. League.org. https://www.league.org/innovation-showcase/breaking-down-barriers-first-generation-college-students-and-college-success

Fitness & Nutrition In College | BestCollegeReviews. (2016, September 15). Www.bestcollegereviews.org. https://www.bestcollegereviews.org/resources/fitness-nutrition-college/

Get the Best Deals on Used Cars For Sale Near Me - Shop Used Cars, Trucks, SUVs and other Vehicles. (n.d.). Edmunds. https://www.edmunds.com/used-cars-for-sale/

Gordon, S. (2021). How to make friends in College. Verywell Family. https://www.verywellfamily.com/how-to-make-friends-in-college-4589

Greene, J. (2023, October 2). How to prioritize tasks when everything feels important. Zapier. https://zapier.com/blog/how-to-prioritize/

Greenwood, W. (2023, April 12). Master Your Time with 20 Effective Tools for Time Management. Priority Management. https://www.prioritymanagement.com.au/tools-for-time-management/

Guardian News and Media. (2013, September 20). *Stories of first-generation students: "I felt dumb, poor and confused" | Dhiya Kuriakose*. The Guardian. https://www.theguardian.com/commentisfree/2013/sep/20/first-generation-college-student-responses

Heineman, E. (2021, May 25). Navigating healthy relationships in college. The Current. https://nsucurrent.nova.edu/2021/05/25/navigating-healthy-relationships-in-college/

Home. (n.d.). College Info Geek. https://collegeinfogeek.com

Home. (n.d.). Edutopia. https://www.edutopia.org

Honors vs. AP Classes: What's the Difference? | BestColleges. (2021, September 8). Www.bestcolleges.com. https://www.bestcolleges.com/blog/honors-vs-ap-classes/

How Do You Know If an Internship Is Right for You? (n.d.). Resources.twc.edu. https://resources.twc.edu/articles/how-do-you-know-if-an-internship-is-right-for-you

How to Balance Life, Work, and School: A Guide for College Students. (n.d.). Purdue Global. https://www.purdueglobal.edu/blog/student-life/work-life-balance-guide-college-students/

How to deal with pressure from your parents. (n.d.). Au.reachout.com. https://au.reachout.com/articles/how-to-deal-with-parents-carers-expectations

How to find a college roommate: 6 tips | BestColleges. (n.d.). BestColleges.com. https://www.bestcolleges.com/blog/how-to-find-a-college-roommate/

How to Improve Self-Knowledge: 21 Books, Tests, & Questions. (2021, August 1). PositivePsychology.com. https://positivepsychology.com/improve-self-knowledge/

How to stay in touch with friends and family | Undergraduate Programs. (2023, February 9). Undergraduate Programs. https://uwaterloo.ca/future-students/missing-manual/student-life/how-stay-touch-friends-and-family

Ideas in Action – University of North Carolina at Chapel Hill. (n.d.). Retrieved October 10, 2023. https://ideasinaction.unc.edu/#:~:text=IDEAs%20in%20Action%20won.

Kelley Blue Book (n.d.). Kelley Blue Book | New and Used Car Price Values, Expert Car Reviews. Kbb.com. https://www.kbb.com/

Kilic, I. (2018, March 29). The Best Workout & Exercise Apps. Medium. https://medium.com/@ihsannkilic/the-best-workout-exercise-apps-23fc60aa5440

Leach, A. (2018, February 14). Not feeling confident? Here are six ways to fake it. The Guardian. https://www.theguardian.com/education/2016/may/18/not-feeling-confident-here-are-six-ways-to-fake-it

Learning, G. (2023, February 6). How to Choose the Right Study Abroad Program?

Lindoph. (2020, January 14). The dos and don'ts of volunteering! DRH Lindersvold. https://lindersvold.dk/the-dos-and-donts-of-volunteering/

Lumen Learning. (2019). https://lumenlearning.com

MD, J. O. (2015, September 2). The 4 Types Of Difficult People And How To Deal With Them. Inspiyr.com. https://inspiyr.com/difficult-people/

Mesrobian, C. (2019, January 24). 11 effective time management tips for college students. Rasmussen University. https://www.rasmussen.edu/student-experience/college-life/time-management-tips-college/

Morin, A. (2022, July 28). 5 ways to start boosting your self-confidence today. Verywell Mind. https://www.verywellmind.com/how-to-boost-your-self-confidence-4163098

Ngo, Chinh. (2014). "Guide to Budgeting in College | BestColleges." BestColleges.com. September 22, 2014. https://www.bestcolleges.com/resources/budgeting-in-college/.

PA, P. P. (2021, February 18). Communicating your priorities better with the "rule of five." Practically Perfect PA. https://www.practicallyperfectpa.com/communicating-your-priorities-better-with-the-rule-of-five/

Paonita, J. (2023). How to Make Friends in College (Even If You're Shy). The Scholarship System. https://thescholarshipsystem.com/blog-for-students-families/how-to-make-friends-in-college-even-if-youre-shy/

Park, J. H., Niu, W., Cheng, L., & Allen, H. (2021). Fostering creativity and critical thinking in college: A cross-cultural investigation. Frontiers in Psychology, 12, 760351.

Pattemore, Chantelle. (2021). "10 Ways to Build and Preserve Better Boundaries." Psych Central. June 3, 2021.

Patterson, R. (2020, June 26). How to Be More Creative (No Matter Your Job or Major). College Info Geek. https://collegeinfogeek.com/how-to-be-creative/

Ph.D. J. N., Ph.D. Tiffany. (2018, January 5). How to Set Healthy Boundaries & Build Positive Relationships. PositivePsychology.com. https://positivepsychology.com/great-self-care-setting-healthy-boundaries/#google_vignette

Pratt Institute. (2022, June 6). 11 Tips for Maintaining a Creative Practice, Even When Home Is Now Your Studio. Pratt Institute. https://www.pratt.edu/news/11-tips-for-maintaining-a-creative-practice-even-when-home-is-now-your-stud/

Progressive Corporation. (2023). How to buy a car as a college student. Progressive.com. https://www.progressive.com/answers/buying-a-car-in-college/

Psych Central. (2022, April 12). Emotion Management Strategies: 6 Methods to Try. https://psychcentral.com/health/ways-to-manage-your-emotions

Ramsdell, D. (2021). Staying Connected With Friends And Family At College — Higher Ed Geek. Higher Ed Geek. https://www.higheredgeek.com/blog/staying-connected-with-friends-and-family-at-college

Rebecca. (2023, June 7). The Top 25 Positive Personality Traits to Adopt. Minimalism Made Simple. https://www.minimalismmadesimple.com/home/positive-personality-traits/

Relationships 101: How to Have Strong College Relationships | Psychology Today. (n.d.). Www.psychologytoday.com. https://www.psychologytoday.com/intl/blog/the-psychology-relationships/202108/relationships-101-how-have-strong-college-relationships

Renting with other people. (n.d.). Citizens Advice. https://www.citizensadvice.org.uk/housing/renting-a-home/renting-with-other-people/

Sandoval, W. (2021, January 21). 8 Tips to Stay Organized In College | BestColleges. BestColleges.com. https://www.bestcolleges.com/blog/tips-to-stay-organized-in-college/

Scott, E. (2020, November 24). The Importance of Self-Care for Health and Stress Management. Verywell Mind; Verywellmind. https://www.verywellmind.com/importance-of-self-care-for-health-stress-management-3144704

Setting Different Types of Career Goals – BigFuture. (2023.). Bigfuture.collegeboard.org. https://bigfuture.collegeboard.org/explore-careers/setting-different-types-career-goals

Sharma, S. (2022, July 1). Exploring creative self-expression (and its importance in our well-being). Calm Sage - Your Guide to Mental and Emotional Well-being. https://www.calmsage.com/creative-self-expression/

Smith, E. W., (n.d.). This Advice Will Make Dating In College So Much Better. Www.refinery29.com. https://www.refinery29.com/en-us/how-to-date-in-college

Staying Healthy in College | Student Wellness Tips | Maryville University. (2019, January 9). Maryville Online. https://online.maryville.edu/blog/exercise-and-nutrition-for-college-students/

Stewart, Irene, and Aaron Maisonville. 2019. "Successful Students Understand Their Finances." Ecampusontario.pressbooks.pub, April. https://ecampusontario.pressbooks.pub/studyprocaff/chapter/successful-students-understand-their-finances/

Swain, R. (2019). The importance of extra-curricular activities | Prospects.ac.uk. Prospects.ac.uk ; Prospects. https://www.prospects.ac.uk/applying-for-university/university-life/the-importance-of-extra-curricular-activities

The Art of Maintaining a Healthy Relationship in College. (n.d.). Www.utep.edu. Retrieved September 26, 2023, from https://www.utep.edu/healthy-miner/resources/the-art-of-maintaining-a-healthy-relationship-in-college.html

The Balancing Act: Managing Multiple Commitments. (2018, January 23). University of Nebraska Omaha. https://www.unomaha.edu/news/2016/03/the-balancing-act-managing-multiple-commitments.php

The Impact of Creativity on College and Career Readiness - EdSurge News. (2023, May 5). Ed-

Surge. https://www.edsurge.com/news/2023-05-05-the-impact-of
-creativity-on-college-and-career-readiness

The Jed Foundation. (2023, September 8). How to Stay
in Touch With Your Family in College | The Jed Founda-
tion. https://jedfoundation.org/resource/how-to-stay-in-touch-wit
h-your-family-in-college/

The Student's Guide to Budgeting in College | BestColleges. (n.d
.). Www.bestcolleges.com.
    https://www.bestcolleges.com/resources/budgeting-in-college/#:
~:text=Additionally%2C%20in%20a%202021%20Sallie.

University of Massachusetts Global. (2020, June 30). How
College Students Can Prioritize Self-Care. Www.brandman.edu
. https://www.umassglobal.edu/news-and-events/blog/self-care-for
-college-students

Warmington, J. (2021, October 4). Five tips for making friends in
college. Boston University. https://www.bu.edu/articles/2021/maki
ng-friends-in-college/

What are the three main types of exercise? | Types Of Exercise.
(2019). Sharecare. https://www.sharecare.com/health/types-exercis
e/what-three-main-types-exercise

Williams, V. (2022). Mayo Clinic Minute: The benefits of being
socially   connected.   Mayo   Clinic   News   Network.
https://newsnetwork.mayoclinic.org/discussion/mayo-clinic-minute
-the-benefits-of-being-socially-connected/#:~:text=Socializing%20no

t%20only%20staves%20off,connecting%20via%20technology%20als
o%20works

Workout ideas for busy students. (September 23, 2023). Hospita
lityinsights.ehl.edu. https://hospitalityinsights.ehl.edu/workout-ide
as-busy-students#:~:text=But%20if%20you%20are%20stuck

You and Your College Experience. (n.d.). 2012books.lardbucket
.org. https://2012books.lardbucket.org/books/success-in-college/s0
4-you-and-your-college-experienc.html

Yousif, M. A., Arbab, A. H., & Yousef, B. A. (2022, February
28). Perceived academic stress, causes, and coping strategies among
undergraduate pharmacy students during the COVID-19 pandemic.
Advances in medical education and practice. https://www.ncbi.nlm
.nih.gov/pmc/articles/PMC8896373/